Fighting Hitler from the
North Jersey Suburbs

Fighting Hitler from the North Jersey Suburbs

By James C. Berrall

BELLE ISLE BOOKS
www.belleislebooks.com

ISBN: 978-1-9399304-0-8

Library of Congress Control Number: 2015934096

Printed in the United States

Published by
BELLE ISLE BOOKS
www.belleislebooks.com
Belle Isle Books, an imprint of Brandylane Publishers, Inc.

For Kim and Julie

"Shoosh! This is *real* footage!"

Preface

I think that the years of World War II must have been my formative years, for they have always stuck with me and I have always been interested in learning more about them. Over the years I have from time to time written down some of my memories of those days and I finally decided to put them together as a narrative. Then I found that, the more I wrote, the more I remembered. The doors just kept popping open.

I've also written this to comment on what I think is a misconception. I think that many people today, particularly young people, have very little idea of what this country was like in the 1940s, especially for kids. I think that much of what we are exposed to about World War II, especially on TV, shows kids being hurt or terrorized—if they appear at all.

For many kids in America, the truth was quite the opposite. Life wasn't bad. We had enough to eat, (and because of less additives, our diet may have even been healthier than what we eat today.) We may have had some holes in our clothes or shoes, but patches and cardboard took care of that. We didn't even think about it because it was the same for us all. We (boys anyhow) certainly did *not* fear air raids or seeing torpedoed ships burning off shore. We never thought we could be hurt; we *wanted* to see something like that. It was *exciting*! It was *fun*!

The America of WWII was vastly different from the America of today. As one who has lived through all of the changes that have come since 1939, I can tell you that to me, the pace of change seems to have been steady most of the time, like the ticking of some inexorable giant clock (or is it a time bomb?). There have been times, though, when the speed has seemed to suddenly jump, to leap ahead as if kicked. The advent of the transistor and the so-called revolution of the sixties come immediately to mind. We accepted these changes as they came, bit by bit; we adjusted to them, and eventually they no longer seemed remarkable and our lives have gone on. The cumulative change has been huge, though, and I think that the average American from 1939 would go into shock if transported suddenly to our time.

To me, the world of my past seems to have been better in many ways. We kids did things then that we can't do anymore. We played outside almost all day, we roamed all about our neighborhoods and sometimes wandered miles away from home without any adult supervision. As long as we didn't get into serious trouble, I don't think our parents worried much.

My mother certainly didn't. This story is also partly about her. My mother was an unusual human being. She had many talents, some of which led her to become a well-known personality in the gardening and flower-arranging fields. She gave talks, guided many tours, both here and in Europe, and authored five books on the subject. Many admired her, greatly respected her, and, I think, put her up on a pedestal of sorts. But my earlier memories of her, which you will read in the following pages, are simpler. They are those of a little boy to whom she was just "Mom" and also one of his best friends.

During the war, the question of who the enemy was was a lot simpler, too. There was no fear of having your legs blown off while watching a sports event, or of having a stray bullet come in the window from a gunfight outside. It was just us and our allies against the bad guys and after the first year we were sure we would beat them.

We were also free of any fear of being bombed, for the oceans on both sides of us were then far too big for almost any bomber to cross. The only people who feared being bombed were, in my opinion, gullible people who had let themselves be spun up by overblown sensational stories and rumors. Except for some rare incidents, in five years the war almost never touched the shores of the United States.

There was no television then, so we rarely got stressed about things like outbreaks of new, unheard-of diseases, possible great howling blizzards or hurricanes, near-misses by gigantic rocks from space, or being swept away in a sudden sea-level rise. We might see brief mention of such things in the newspapers, but the real news was always about the war—and by 1943, it was almost always good.

I feel that I have been lucky in several ways. One of them is my age. I, along with almost all of my friends (many of whom are guys I was in Cub Scouts with), was born at a time that kept me out of the wars. We've been out of sync: too young for World War II, exempt from Korea for one reason or another, too old for Vietnam, and then too old for any of the little wars since then.

I have always felt very fortunate in where I grew up. Although it had a few somewhat threadbare sections, Montclair in general was and is considered an affluent suburb. My early environment was certainly not one of poverty (though I was quite aware from time to time that money was tight). Several of my hometown friends and I have often remarked on how lucky we were to grow up when and where we did.

My home's location in that town made me more fortunate still. My father was an architect and he carefully picked out the piece of land he wanted to build our house on. It was up on the highest western edge of town, so I grew up able to see it and the surrounding area spread out below me, all the way to the Atlantic. That included New York City. At night it was particularly impressive.

In the other direction, to the west—and perhaps having had an even greater effect on me—were rock cliffs and, on top of them, woods that extended for miles. I grew up climbing on rocks and running through the woods trying to be like Tarzan. It left me with a lifelong love of the outdoors, particularly rocks and forests.

Flying intrigued me from a very early age. I recall being fascinated as a little boy sometime before the war by watching a skywriter slowly making a gigantic letter "P" in the sky—the beginning of the word "Pepsi."

With the onset of the Battle of Britain, the fighter pilots of the RAF became the greatest heroes of our time and stories about their exploits were everywhere. I decided (like everyone else) that I was going to be a fighter pilot then, and followed that ambition into the Air Force some years later. I learned how to fly, but a fascination with science fiction had started at an early age, too. In fifth grade, sitting on a little stool in the library, I read H. G. Wells's *War of the Worlds*, and I was hooked. Also, some early stories by Robert Heinlein, a science fiction writer who later became quite famous, started to appear in the *Saturday Evening Post* and left an indelible mark on me. I wanted to go into space, but we weren't doing that yet, and the closest thing to it was guided missiles. After some maneuvering, I was accepted for the first class of Air Force ICBM Launch Officers and served for the remainder of my tour as the commander of a missile launch crew. After leaving active duty, I was employed for some time in the rocket propulsion field and, later on, in ballistic missile interception. I've also worked as an illustrator for several years for Goddard Space Flight Center.

I changed directions sometime later and worked as the assistant director of a Civil War Battlefield Museum. My interest in military history was undoubtedly fostered by my early years during WWII, but while the field has surely interested me, I am the opposite of a "war lover." I have learned enough about the horrors of war (and, having been a SAC launch control officer, that does include thermonuclear war—which actually means "suicide") that I want no part of one and am eternally thankful to have missed them all.

So far.

1939 – 40

CHAPTER 1

The Gates of Warsaw

Okay, get comfy—get that heavy steel can of Ballantine's out of the icebox . . . don't forget the church key; pull tabs haven't been invented yet. Better get a coaster with a rim to put under it—it's gonna sweat a lot and there isn't any air conditioning, either. Yeah, light up a Chesterfield, too. No, of course it's not filtered. Whaddaya want? Something like Roosevelt uses? A big long cigarette holder? Whadda laugh!

My earliest memory of World War II is from the month it started: September, 1939. I was riding in the back seat of the family Ford V-8 sedan, going north on the Merritt Parkway in Connecticut. We were on our way to see my aunt (my mother's sister), uncle, and their two sons in their old farmhouse west of Hartford. It was hot, and I was nauseated (which my mother called "feeling icky in the garden"), and I had a slight headache the whole way because of the heat and the fumes.

There were plenty of fumes in those days. Most cars made blue smoke that you could both see and smell. It stank. No catalytic converters, no air conditioning. And the adults in the front seat wondered why we got carsick.

The back seat fabric was scratchy on the backs of my bare legs.

I was wearing shorts. I was five.

The adults were talking about the Germans invading Poland, and you could tell it was serious by the sound of their voices. It sounded as if Germans were almost as bad as "weavers" or "Sunday drivers."

I was sure I knew what Poland looked like, because in Connecticut I could see poles in all the fields right outside the car windows. Lots of tall black poles, twelve feet high, sticking up everywhere.

The radio had said that the Germans were "at the gates of Warsaw," and

I was pretty sure I knew what those looked like, too: big, black, filigreed iron gates with tall, vertical bars, pointed on top with plenty of scrollwork. I had seen them somewhere, possibly when I had gone along with my father on one of his jobs. He was an architect.

I kept urging him to drive faster, to go 60—a mile a minute (which sounded exciting), so that I could see what it was like. He did edge up there once, uneasily, to appease me, but that was it. My father liked to stay at 55 or below. He had a great respect for the law and a vast, snarling distaste for what he called "weavers," which were those people who, driven nearly mad by slow people in the fast lane, wove in and out, trying to find some clear air.

Mostly he told me to keep quiet.

My grandfather (my mother's father), was with us, too. He was my mentor. He had started teaching me to read when I was two, which gave me a bit of an edge on my schoolmates later on. He also had a vast collection of tools and trinkets and fascinating pictures and articles clipped out of magazines, as well as a collection of old firearms, which I naturally wanted to get my hands on, but was rarely allowed to touch. I think firearms are like magnets to any young boy.

I've been told I'm a lot like my grandfather. "You're so much like him it gives me the creeps!" my mother once said. "You even blow your nose like he does!"

Well, duh. Who do you suppose I was copying? I liked to do it his way because it was a loud, satisfying, "Honk!" instead of something more genteel.

There was no such thing as "political correctness" then. If a parent didn't want their kid to do something, the kid would be asked, then told, not to do it, in escalating degrees of "serious voice," all the way up to whatever would happen when your father got home. Sometimes that could be pretty painful.

What *was* common was a thing called "politeness"—a tool that could be used in many different ways. At one extreme, for instance, I think I have seen some bygone movie star, Bette Davis or Joan Crawford perhaps, utter a polite phrase with such exquisite, sarcastic sweetness as to put a real burner on someone, a slight the person could not comfortably respond to.

This was not done by people my age, by the way. If you tried it, you might regret it.

The old farmhouse in Connecticut was owned by my uncle and aunt and was, for the U.S., really old, built in 1760. I've never experienced Thanksgiving in a better place. It could make you feel like you were in a movie about pilgrims. If you were there at the right time of year and had just eaten a lot of turkey with stuffing and some cranberry jelly, drunk some cider, and the remains of a small fire were dying down in the big fireplace—if there were perhaps a cold drizzle falling and you quickly turned your head, you might briefly think you had seen a small ghostly band of Mohawk Indians creeping through the misty woods.

The floorboards of the house were all different widths—some as much as a foot wide—and they creaked when you walked on them. The old fireplace was big enough to walk into and had a small bench to one side where you could sit beside the fire to get warm. There were big, old, black cooking utensils hanging here and there also.

In the corner of the living room there was a narrow staircase that went up to the second floor. One of the bedrooms right over the living room had a circular hole cut in the floor to let the hot air come up. That hole fascinated me and was a little worrisome, too. What if you misjudged and stepped in it? It had a cover, but I didn't trust it.

Coming down to breakfast in the mornings, I would always smell a pleasant, pungent odor as I turned the corner on the stairs. Years later, my cousin Ted told me that the smell was kerosene that had soaked into a bed of sawdust from a big barrel that had sat for many years in a corner of the room beneath. Ted long had the job, first thing in the morning, of getting a small pail of kerosene from the barrel, taking it into the kitchen, filling the hot water heater fuel tank, and lighting it off so that the family had hot water. That smell was always there and I liked it a lot. Some years later, I encountered that smell again, on just about every air force or civilian runway I've ever been near.

Jet engine breath has always reminded me of that old farmhouse.

By 1939, anybody who hadn't buried his head in the sand could see that war was coming. Talk about war and guns and airplanes and battleships was everywhere. I think we were exposed to a lot more of it than we had been in years prior. And it's been that way ever since.

The grown-ups talked about the war some, but not much that I recall. They probably thought that it would scare us children. But I think they were projecting their own concerns onto us. We young boys were fascinated by *anything* to do with war. But the adults had experienced a war already, only twenty-one years before. That must have been somewhat depressing for them.

A lot of what grown-ups talk about sails right over kids' heads because it just isn't relevant to a kid's world. But there was one time when, talking about what-ifs concerning the war, my aunt ventured an opinion, and my uncle, who sometimes seemed to exhibit a haughtiness worthy of a stereotypical New Englander, said in an exasperated tone, "Oh, nonsense, Dorothy!"

This got my attention. In the first place, I had never heard an adult say something like that to another adult; and in the second place, I had thought her name was "Spot." How she got that nickname I didn't know, but I had always heard her referred to as "Aunt Spot." A further confusing thing was that I later saw *The Wizard of Oz* and got my aunt and the Dorothy in the movie sort of mixed up in my mind for a while. But their dog's name was Skippy, not Toto. He didn't look at all like Toto either.

Skippy would lie on the floor at my uncle's feet as he read the evening paper, and whenever my uncle read something he disagreed with (perhaps some "nonsense" dreamed up by Washington) he would make a growling noise indicating distaste, sort of like "Unnngarrrmmm." Whereupon Skippy, lying on the floor at his feet, would heave a deep sigh and also say, "Unnnngarrrrmmm!"

I thought it was pretty funny, but I was careful not to laugh.

We cousins became good friends. Ted was the oldest by a year and a half. I was next, then Ted's brother, Bob, who was two years younger than me, then my brother, Pete, who was a year younger than Bob. Bob was called "Robin" in those days by everyone, but it seems he did not care for that name and later insisted that he be called Bob. Well, that was O.K. by me. In fact, I completely understand it, but this seems a good time to mention that one of the most competent, tiger-like, aggressive, legendary fighter pilot aces to ever fly for the U.S. Air Force was also named Robin: General Robin Olds. I think if anyone had ever had the bad judgment to make fun of his name, he might have torn them into little pieces to feed to his pet falcon.

The farm in Connecticut was not a working farm; it was just a good investment and also a nice place to retreat to in the summer. My aunt did grow vegetables and "put them up" in jars, but that was a long way from being the family's main source of sustenance. Later on (two and a half years later on), after we got into the war and rationing was imposed, vegetable gardens became more important and lots of people had them. They were then called "Victory Gardens," and if you had one, you could take pride in it and hold your head up because you were "doing your part." And you could lord it over your friends a little bit, too.

My mother had one, naturally, and I was theoretically part owner of a small piece of it. I had to weed my section and kill bugs and learn to grow things. Since a good part of the crop was string beans, I was less than motivated. I did learn some useful things about planting and growing, though. I still grow tomatoes and pumpkins, and since I have a very sincere pumpkin patch, I am still hoping to be visited by you-know-who and if you don't, you need to brush up on your Peanuts.

I also learned that to get things to grow in your Victory Garden, you had to make a sign that had on it a "V" and three dots and a dash, all drawn in red, white, and blue, with stars in the blue part.

That really did help. Things started to grow after I put up that sign.

Mom also had a flower garden. Our house was on a curve in the road, and the whole circular front of the yard was devoted to her garden, in which something would be blooming almost year round. The road normally had very little traffic, but on weekends, particularly Sundays, there were often people driving slowly around the curve, looking out their windows. I didn't think much about it at the time, but they certainly irritated my father. I doubt he realized that some of them were probably there to ogle Mom's flower garden. "Sunday Drivers," he would growl with vast distaste whenever he saw one roll slowly by.

There was another trip we made around this time, to a place on the Rhode Island coast called Haversham. It was surrounded by towns with Indian names like Weekapaug and Quonochontaug. The house we were going to was on a rise on the landward side of a tidal lagoon maybe half a mile wide. On the far side was a thin stretch of barrier beach, then the ocean. The house was exactly what you might expect of the old New England coast. It was low and gray and weathered, obscured on the inland side by trees and great tangles of thorny vines. It had a sort of linear layout with many rooms. It looked like it had been there for over a hundred years, which it probably had.

My mother had many fond childhood memories of that place, where, in the summers, she and her sister and another pair of female cousins had spent many hours on the beach and paddling or sailing around. It belonged to one of those cousins and her husband, who was the brother of Ted and Bob's father. They had a daughter who was older than any of us, and a son, Philip, who was younger than me and older than Bob, so we five boys were a stair-stepped progression of cousins from youngest to oldest. Confusing? Oh yeah. As a kid I could never get it straight (and I never really tried to). Besides that, there were various other aunts and cousins mixed into the equation.

It may well be that I still don't have it right.

It was either on this trip, or somewhere on the trip to the farm, that we spotted three big sailing ships in a harbor, several miles away. In my memory they are almost on the horizon, because I can still see the most impressive thing about them: two of them had five masts, and the third one had six! I am not certain, but I believe that a six-masted schooner was somewhat rare even in the golden age of great sailing ships. That had to be some clankin' big ship and under full sail—quite a sight!

It could be that I saw them at Bridgeport, or somewhere around New London. I think they were there all through the war, but toward the end, only the two five-masters were there. Maybe the six-masted one was used for the timber in it, maybe for firewood (it would have made a lot of firewood, and during the war, firewood was a good thing to have). Maybe it just rotted and sank in place. I dunno, but it was gone.

That first visit to Haversham was only a year after the great hurricane of 1938. There were still some signs of wreckage and a lot of fresh memories. The adults talked more about the hurricane than about the war. A lot more. They had a big book—I guess we would now call it a "coffee table book"— done in sepia tone, that was full of photos of various scenes of the hurricane's destruction. The images of houses displaced hundreds, or even thousands, of feet from where they belonged fascinated me.

People talked a lot about the "tidal wave" that came with the hurricane, too. Or maybe it just fascinated me. Now we call it a "storm surge," but in any case, it seems to have been a very large one. Weather forecasting was nowhere near as advanced then as it is today, and the unusually fast-moving hurricane and its storm surge had taken a lot of people by surprise. Some lucky ones had even lived through water-borne rides of several miles. Many others had not been so lucky. I believe the total death toll was up around six hundred.

Tidal wave paranoia lasted for several years. There is a movie called *Portrait of Jenny*, made after the hurricane, in which "the wave" virtually becomes the central character in the last reel and is presented in a downright terrifying manner.

A popular song at the time was titled "Three Little Fishes," but we called it "Boop Boop Didddum Daddum Waddem Choo," which was a phrase repeated several times in the song. We kids liked the sound of that, thought it was very funny, and used it too much. The adults probably got real tired of it.

The song was popular for at least two reasons: first, because it was a nonsense song (a genre becoming more and more fashionable then but which had yet to produce "Mairsy Doats," an all-time doubletalk winner); and second, because at the end, "They swam and they swam right over the dam."

Ooh! Ooh! Ooh! Really pushin' it there, you see, because they actually said "dam" out loud on the radio!

We've come a long way.

Another song that became really popular—for several reasons, but mostly with kids because it had some vulgar sounds in it—was "The Fuhrer's Face." It had the sound of someone breaking wind loudly after each "Heil," so it went: "So ven der Fuhrer says, 've are der master race,' ve Heil, (*framp!*) Heil, (*framp!*) right in der fuhrer's face!"

It struck us kids (and I imagine anyone who disagreed with Nazi philosophy) as hugely funny. It sounds pretty funny to me even now. I think Spike Jones recorded it; he did lots of songs with sound effects in them. It made for quite effective counter-propaganda. I imagine that song could have driven any serious member of the Nazi Party into a red-faced, screaming, spittle-flinging spit-fit.

The Nazis and Hitler had been getting more and more worrisome in the preceding years, as they annexed country after country around them, always on some trumped-up excuse. They might claim, for instance, that the people they had taken over were actually ethnic Germans and welcomed being assimilated into Hitler's Reich; or they might say that the territory was really Germany's but had been taken away by the Armistice following the last war. People all over the world were getting more and more upset about this kind of thing and were beginning to think that maybe this buffoon, this nut Hitler was really going to cause some serious trouble. But many others, especially in the U.S., just couldn't take him—with his little toothbrush mustache—seriously. And many other Americans were extremely serious about *not* wanting us to get involved again in another of Europe's seemingly endless series of wars.

But after a lull of several months, having become convinced that France and England lacked the backbone to ever do anything to stop him, Hitler attacked Poland on a trumped-up excuse and then it was "Here we go again!" Britain and France, sadly and reluctantly honoring treaties they had made, declared war on Germany but took very little action at all. Russia, which had previously signed a pact with Hitler, helped him divide up Poland and occupied most of Poland's eastern half.

Even though they were technically at war, Britain and France just sort of sat out the winter of '39. There was some air activity, but it was largely devoted to dropping leaflets on Germany, urging them to play nice and to stop being so naughty. Very few bombs were dropped, because nobody wanted to stir things up and make Hitler mad.

One of the British air ministers was actually heard to say (concerning a proposal to use incendiary bombs to set fire to a famous German forest), "Are you aware that that is private property? Why, you'll be asking me to bomb Essen next!"

Before the war was over, Essen would become the most frequently bombed city in Germany.

But perhaps the air minister knew what he was doing. The British desperately needed time to build up their air force. The Spitfire was the only RAF (Royal Air Force) fighter that could match the Messerschmitt 109, and very few had yet been built. The famous Merlin engine that powered them and so many other allied aircraft, including our famous P-51, also needed more development time. The Merlin, in fact, might never have been developed in time at all if it had not been for the convenient gift, some years before, of £100,000 by a relatively unknown and unsung heroine of British history, Lady Houston. (That gift, surely the equivalent of several million dollars today, may have actually won WWII for us. I hope there is a monument somewhere that honors her.)

In the end the Merlin was developed just in time to power the British Hurricanes and Spitfires that were able to fight the German Luftwaffe to a standstill in the Battle of Britain. It's hard to guess what might have happened if they had failed, but it is certainly possible that we might live in an entirely different world today.

This early period of the war was called "The Phony War" and, in some places, the "Sitzkrieg." A fairly famous picture of a French soldier sitting in a chair at his guard post on the French-German border appeared in *Life* magazine and may have contributed to that title.

I must have been pre-kindergarten at that time, so there aren't too many memories available, but I do remember that trip to Connecticut and the Nazis being at the gates of Warsaw.

Chapter 2

Battleships and Ghosts

In kindergarten, at "nap time," we had to lie on our little mats or rugs on the floor. On the *floor*? Yes, on the floor. I had never tried to sleep on the floor before. (Probably I had, but I just couldn't remember it.) I remember that my little rug was green and that it was hard to keep still. I certainly didn't nap. Instead, my classmates and I sneaked looks and made weird signals to each other. Sometimes we might roll things like marbles across the floor, too, but that would only work once and maybe not at all. Mrs. Shaw was pretty sharp. She seemed to have good ears, too.

There was a little girl in that class with whom I was in love. Her name was Louise, and she was blond and vivacious. She was certainly cute, but the thing that for a while made her overwhelmingly popular (which for a kid is like winning the lottery) was that while running, then sliding, down a long hall in their house, she and her sister had collided, and she had bit her tongue and had to have it sewed up. They "put a stitch" in it. So any time you asked her to, she would obligingly tilt her head back and, grinning a great grin, stick out her tongue to proudly show off her single, big, black stitch. It was startling. I can still see her doing it.

I also remember a blue and green plaid skirt she often wore. It had a *big* silver safety pin halfway down that appeared to hold it together and you had to wonder what would happen if the pin ever popped open. That was another thing that made her fascinating.

Louise has also told me that one of her fond kindergarten memories is of sneaking up and kissing me on the back of the neck. To my eternal shame, I must admit that I only hazily remember that fabulous event.

Now, here is something that I think may be a little unusual: An unbelievable number of years have passed (*zip!*). Louise is still fascinating, still my dear friend, and I still love her. She grew up and married a guy who has also been my dear friend for almost as long. She is the friend I have had longest in life.

That kindergarten class was seventy-five years ago.

Another close friend of mine was a girl named Nancy. Her house was at the far end of my street, but across Bradford Avenue, which was a broad curve going downhill. Cars were apt to be unseen and moving fast when they popped around that downhill curve—you had to have an adult with you to cross.

"But *why* can't I cross by myself?"

"Because it's too dangerous."

"But nothing's coming."

"You just can't. Don't argue with me!"

Now, thinking back, I realize that it surely was dangerous, and that the parents were absolutely right. Thinking of my own kids doing that—on their tricycles—is a genuinely scary thought. On the other hand, that's nothin'. Just wait till I tell you about "cliff tag."

Nance and I were the only kids in the neighborhood who were the same age. Her older brother, Jackie, was about four years my senior, and he and I did a lot of climbing and throwing rocks in the old abandoned quarry that was just up the street from my house. We drew a lot of pictures, too.

Nance and I must have done lots of things together, but I can recall only a few of them. One thing that has stuck in my mind was that we would dip our barley-sugar lollipops, shaped like horses and roosters, into snow banks, and after a while, we'd take them out and eat them, because they were much better when cold and covered with snow and ice. I still consider the taste special. Real Lowenbrau beer will give you that wonderful barley aftertaste. Their dark beer is best, but it has to be real—imported from Bavaria, not that stuff that comes from a horse somewhere near Dallas.

I also recall some tricycle crashes resulting in abrasions that would require the attention of someone's mother and then (argh!) *iodine*! That was the worst part—the iodine. You knew it was gonna hurt worse than the original wound. (I wonder why we didn't just try to cover up the evidence of a cut? Probably we were so indoctrinated that we believed if you didn't sterilize a cut your leg would fall off.)

"*Stop crying!* Be a man about it!" But you did make a sort of high, whining noise because you knew the iodine sting was coming.

"*Stop crying!*" And you'd try. You'd really try. You'd clamp your teeth and close your lips tight and what would come out was a noise like

"Nnnnnnnnuuuuuuuuungh! Nnnnnnnnnnnummmgh!" like you might hear coming from behind a closed bathroom door. Sometimes that sounded so funny that you might start to laugh, which could make you angry because you were supposed to be crying.

It was hard, but it was early training in stoicism, and I think it had some lasting effect. (You knew you would be in combat and would probably be wounded sooner or later—maybe captured, and they were sure to torture you to make you talk.) I have been left, at any rate, with a certain amount of contempt for people who wail and howl over a little pain.

I also seem to have been left with a subconscious distrust of antiseptics that don't sting—a deep-seated, lurking suspicion that the stuff isn't quite doing the job. With iodine you knew it damn well was! It felt like you'd dropped acid in the cut. It *had* to be hard on them germs! Probably burning and disintegrating them. Of course, now we know that iodine on a cut kills about eight times more cells than the cut itself and is worse than just cleaning it, covering it, and leaving it alone, but then it was accepted as state-of-the-art home-battlefield trauma treatment.

Just to be sure those who were never there appreciate my point, please do me this little favor. Next time you do some little thing to yourself that draws blood, pour a little whiskey or vodka or even aftershave on it. Then you'll better understand why we didn't like iodine!

There were two other older kids who lived in other houses up Bradford Avenue, too, but they were both a little bit "weird" and we didn't interact. They were different, withdrawn, standoffish. One of them later got in some serious trouble for "breaking and entering" into houses in the neighborhood, but that was just for the excitement and challenge of it, you know, not for looting in particular. It was just to prove they could actually do it, which is something I completely understand.

(But just try explaining *that* to your parents . . . or the police!)

Sometime around the beginning of the war, my father gave me some pencils with big, soft pencil lead in them and you could certainly draw some heavy dark lines with them. I was much into speedboats for a while and I drew a lot of them, noses tilted up impossibly high with huge banks of spray and rooster tails shooting out. I have been somewhat amazed these days to see real speedboats doing exactly what I was drawing! I even drew one not touching the water, just howling along with the propeller still submerged—and so help me, I saw one actually doing just that on the tube the other day!

Sometime in 1939 or 1940 my parents took me on an excursion to New

York because "the fleet was in." It can't have been the whole fleet, probably just the Atlantic squadron, but it was a lot of ships. A lot of *big* ships. Some of them were actual *battleships*, and that was really exciting to me. I was very turned on by battleships then. Still am, actually.

I still believe that there is nothing so impressively gigantic and powerful, yet at the same time so sweeping and graceful as an Iowa-class battleship. Nothing.

But the Iowas hadn't been built yet. What we saw that day were battleships of the prewar navy that had been built around the time of the First World War. They were slowly being modernized but were a long way from being in the same league as, say, the *Bismarck*.

We were taken out to tour one, the USS *New York*. I remember being impressed by what looked like a big clock face on the front mast, just above the bridge. I asked a sailor what it was for, but I don't think I got a very satisfactory answer. You can see those clock faces on battleship pictures from those times, but I still don't know what they were for. Maybe showing elapsed time during drills of some kind? I dunno.

I was also very curious about what looked like a big, flat, bedspring at the top of the mast. I asked a sailor about that, too, and he told me that it was a new kind of radio aerial—and smiled sort of knowingly as he said it. Now I know that it was an early radar antenna. The *New York* was the first ship in the fleet to experimentally mount one. This was "secret" technology that the British were experimenting with and were sharing with us. Within a year, they would be using similar "bedspring" antennas mounted on 350-foot-high towers to detect German air raids assembling at more than a hundred miles' distance. The towers were placed in an unbroken line all around the British coast.

It is quite possible that without them there may have been a completely different outcome to the war, for the British, in their planning, had assumed they would be attacked by airplanes coming all the way from Germany, not the recently conquered coast of France.

After touring the *New York*, we went over to see the *Langley*. *Langley* was our first aircraft carrier. It had been created by putting a flight deck on top of the old collier *Jupiter*. It was really a pretty slap-dash aircraft carrier, but it did carry airplanes and conducted many early naval experiments concerning carrier techniques and operations.

A strong, lasting image that has stayed printed on my memory from that visit is of a big, tall sailor with curly black hair who was answering some of my questions and how long and thick (like tree-trunks) his white-uniformed legs looked, extending way up in the air above me. There were long afternoon sunbeams slanting down on us because we were down on the hanger deck among the tall girders that held the flight deck up. I've never forgotten that scene or the big sailor, because he was so friendly to me.

Langley was sunk in battle in the Java Sea two years later. I hope that big sailor made it.

We also made a trip to the Hayden Planetarium at the Museum of Natural History in New York. I was greatly impressed by the motorized planets going around in their tracks on the ceiling overhead and the big Ahnighito Meteorite, a lump of pitted nickel-iron as big as a small car (stolen from the Inuit by Admiral Peary), sitting proudly on its pedestal in the entrance hall.

It was announced that the show was about to begin, so we went in and found seats. I had never before seen seats that tilted backwards to give the occupant a better view of the ceiling, which was hard to see and seemed to be far away. The large, circular, dimly lit theater seemed vast. The floor sloped away, down toward the center, where a big, weird-looking machine rose up on a pedestal. It appeared to be covered with eyes and seemed to me to be staring down at the audience.

Then quiet and peaceful symphonic music slowly became noticeable, coming from all directions. City buildings were silhouetted all around the horizon of the auditorium, and they became more and more distinct as the lights gradually dimmed. I don't remember the rest of the show, but the reason I had wanted so much to go was that they were having a special presentation about a trip to Mars in a spaceship. The great room darkened, and projected on the ceiling were the silhouettes of two pilots, seated at what I now think was the instrument panel of a DC-3. They were wearing what looked like regular airline pilots' hats with visors, and even then that didn't seem right to me. The flight progressed, the narrator told us we were about to land and . . . WHAM! There was a loud noise and a shockingly bright flash of light as all the auditorium lights flashed (scary!) and then, with a grinding noise, the hatch was opened. We saw a desert scene where *everything* was pink—sky and sand, all bright pink! And—EGAD! Something . . . a *giant grasshopper* was peering in at us!

Oh, it was an amazing, wonderful show. For a five-year-old.

The whole experience generated a lifelong love of planetariums in me, and whenever I hear low, soothing symphonic music now, I think of it as "planetarium music."

Late in 1939 there was a great to-do about a German "Pocket Battleship," the *Graf Spee*. The Germans had built several of these ships and were using them effectively as commerce raiders. The theory was that their eleven-inch guns were powerful enough to sink anything they couldn't outrun and that they were fast enough to outrun anything too big to outshoot. They were diesel-powered, could go 12,000 miles before refueling, and roamed the seas alone, looking for British merchantmen and ships of their trading partners to attack and sink. They were very much a thorn in the side of the British Navy, which covered the oceans of the world with groups of warships looking for the raiders. Finally they found the *Graf Spee* in the South Atlantic, and HMS *Ajax*, *Achilles*, and *Exeter* took her on. "*Ajax*, *Achilles*, and *Exeter*" was a phrase I remember hearing a lot at the time.

All three British ships were outgunned, but they gave as good as they got. The *Graf Spee* ran for shelter at Montevideo, but was told she had to leave within two days. The clever British had used their radios to convince the Germans that many British big-gun battleships were outside waiting for her, so she sailed out into the river and her captain ordered her scuttled. A photograph of the ship, partly collapsed and burning, became somewhat famous. My father reproduced the picture in soft pencil on paper for us, and the way he represented the smoke billowing out in different shades fascinated me for years. The things he could do with a pencil were impressive.

Sometime in 1940, two British refugees, a mother and daughter who were related to us through my father's sister's husband, came to America. At that time it was possible for people in England, if they had relatives in the States, to come over here to escape the bombing. I think it was particularly to get the children away.

My mother, who was outspokenly in favor of the British (an opinion *not* held by at least half the population of the U.S.) immediately tried to do everything she could to help the two and make them feel welcome. It soon became the custom for them to come to our house on Sunday mornings to eat breakfast with us and spend the rest of the day.

Miesje, the daughter, was my age. She remembers that the playwright Noel Coward had also come over on their ship, and that the next ship after theirs, also filled with little kids, was torpedoed and sunk.

There was a time I remember when Miesje and I were put to bed in an unfamiliar room at someone else's house. We were in separate beds in the same room, and of course we were hyped-up and talked a lot. We stayed awake for quite a while talking about ghosts (we were constantly told that there was "no such thing as ghosts," but like all sensible kids, we weren't entirely convinced). Miesje was sure she knew what they looked like: she said they had trunks, like elephants. She seemed to know, so I just accepted this as fact. We drew many pictures of ghosts with trunks, and they do seem more creepy that way! Draw a picture of one, you'll see. But I wonder if that idea could have come from the gas masks the soldiers wore in the trenches in World War I, with the corrugated hose that led down from the mask to the charcoal canister? The question then becomes, did she see a picture of this somewhere that gave her the idea, or did she see something else? Or was it something the kids in England told each other? The British lost an awful lot of men during WWI.

We also talked about what to do if something *really* bad were to happen. Like, for instance, if a *real* ghost did come out of the closet or something. I planned on hunkering down in the bed and pulling the covers up over my head, but she was sure that the best place to go was under the bed. What? Get out of bed and go on the cold floor under it where whatever it was could get your bare feet and legs? Not me, no way, no thanks!

But she was absolutely certain about it. I see now that she would have been told to do that in England because of bombs and the potential for collapsing ceilings. Still, at the time there was nothing so scary as a ghost.

CHAPTER 3

The World of Tomorrow

The 1939 New York World's Fair had been held over for a second year, so in 1940, we had a big expedition to go see it.

I didn't know what to expect, but when we got there, the amazement started. First off, you didn't have to walk all the time; there were a lot of little trains of about six open cars on rubber wheels that went all over the place, to all the exhibits. They all had melodic horns that went "doo-dee, doo-dee" all the time, everywhere. I can still hear them.

We went to the railroad exhibit, and while I was impressed by the huge, modern locomotives, I was even more impressed by the great wide beds of crushed white stones as big as ice-cubes, dazzling in the sunlight, that had been put down to lay the tracks on. By that time I had soaked up a little geology from my grandfather and I thought the white stone was milky quartz. Gold is often found associated with quartz, but I couldn't find any.

Then we went to an exhibit in the AT&T building, where there was a robot. I really wanted to see a robot. I think the robot's name was "Voder." He was about the size of a big man but very clunky looking. I think he could move, but not much. Voder could talk, sort of, but his lips didn't move. His words were created by a lady who picked them out on a keyboard that looked just like our piano keyboard at home. I was not much impressed by Voder. The Tin Woodman in *The Wizard of Oz* looked a lot more realistic than Voder did.

The Trylon and Perisphere together were the official symbol of the 1939 World's Fair. The Trylon was a three-sided obelisk, seven hundred feet high, tapering thinly to its top, and the Perisphere was a big white sphere, two hundred feet in diameter, sitting on the ground right next to it. The logo of a ball and obelisk were printed on *everything* that had anything to do with the

16

World's Fair. The Perisphere was hollow. That was where you went to see "The World of Tomorrow."

Now, *that* was something that really caught the attention of this six-year old! Inside the huge ball was a ramp circling all around the inside wall. From it, we could see below us a panorama of the world of the future, which predicted many things that have actually come about (and many which have not). I may have a lot of this mixed up in my mind with a diorama I saw at the General Motors exhibit, but in one of them, I saw great wide highways soaring above the park-like land, highways filled with vehicles whistling along at amazing speeds. The buildings were smooth and futuristic looking, and there were big airliners flying across the sky. Huge airliners with eight engines, but with straight wings and propellers on the engines!

Some things are hard to predict. (The only true jet engines in the world at the time were both experimental and secret, one in England and one in Germany.)

Of course, nobody had even thought of anything like the transistor yet, and as for lasers, well, I guess H. G. Wells' Martian heat ray was about as close as anyone had yet come to predicting that.

I don't remember much more about the World's Fair except that at some exhibit, I got a huge copper Indian-head penny. I remember it as being about four inches in diameter. I had to hold it with both hands because it was so heavy. I don't know what happened to it—it probably disappeared somehow into one of my "friends'" collections of geegaws. At that age, we were all pretty light-fingered with each other's property, be it comic books, toy soldiers, decoder badges, etc.

Years later, I saw another one of those pennies—I don't remember in what context, but it wasn't a World's Fair. This one was only about two inches in diameter, but it was the same coin. I suppose my hands had grown bigger, but still, it didn't seem right.

I have read that in the fair's second year, many of the original fair exhibits were gone, closed down because of the war. Some of the sponsoring countries had been invaded or were preparing to avoid invasion. But I didn't know of or notice any shortcomings. I thought the whole fair was a magical, wonderful place, with broad, open streets, statues, and futuristic-looking buildings. I never got to see it at night, but from pictures I've seen, it must have been fantastic.

Sadly, what actually came next was not the "World of Tomorrow" portrayed by the fair, but a world of war.

I say "sadly," but it wasn't sad for us kids—not at all! It was actually quite interesting most of the time, and sometimes it could get downright exciting.

It was a good time for many of our parents, too. They were just emerging from a crushing economic depression and it was beginning to look like there would be some opportunity again.

Years later, I asked a friend, John Roberts, who was one of my favorite teachers in high school, what it had been like for him and his friends when the war came: how did it change his life?

"There was a lot more money and sex," he said. So that kind of gives you some perspective.

Even many people in England, where there was a real possibility of getting maimed or killed, will say that they now realize the war years were the best of their lives, that they have never felt so alive since. People were full of adrenaline and had a common purpose. It was an exciting time, a *great* time (if you weren't getting shot at)! We should also remember that in England, things were pretty grim for many years after the war.

For me, during 1940 and most of 1941, I was mostly concerned with pictures in magazines and the Sunday paper. I collected airplane and battleship pictures and sometimes caught some flak because I had cut a picture out before people were finished reading the magazine.

These were times when the summer days felt long and it seemed that summer would last forever. (Remember that at that age, one year is a fifth of a kid's whole life). There were all sorts of amazing, wonderful things going on. Cousin Ted and I once caught lightning bugs and put them in a covered jar in our room at night for the fascinating, flickering light show. We both had Jack Armstrong glow-in-the-dark Dragon's Eye rings and waved them around with the fireflies while we were supposed to be going to sleep. Then we awoke the next morning to find the fireflies all dead on the bottom of the jar—we didn't know enough to punch holes in the top to give them air.

Sometimes during the summer, Mom would take an orange, cut a hole in the top just big enough to push a sugar lump down in, and give it to us to suck on while we squeezed the juice out into our mouths. (Clever! I may at this time have been resisting drinking orange juice at breakfast.) I wonder if moms still do this? Probably not, since it has become well-known modern dietary correct-think that sugar is a deadly poison.

Those oranges, however, were damn good. Cool, sweet, and juicy on a hot summer day! I wish I had one right now.

Another thing that was damn good were "sugar jumbles" (or were they jumbos?). I dunno, I've always remembered them as "jumbles," but the other would make sense because they were *big* cookies, a quarter of an inch thick, bigger around than doughnuts, and with a hole in the middle, too. I think they were ginger cookies, but they may have been molasses. They were not hard, but that may have been because they were really fresh. They came from either Marker's or Hassler's, two stores that probably did all their own baking on premises. It really smelled good in those stores. And the surprising thing about those cookies, the thing that made them so special, was that they were covered all over with big individual sugar crystals. The crystals were cubes about an eighth of an inch on each side. Those cookies were amazing! And they must have been fairly expensive, too, because we didn't get to have them very often. Sometimes I could, by intense whining, persuade Mom to get some, but more often it was she who would say, with a smile like a friendly fellow conspirator, "Hey, do you want to get some sugar jumbles?"

Of course, she knew what my answer would be.

Do stores where they do their own baking still exist? (I bet they do, but only in the rich people's places where we aren't allowed to go—Economics 101.)

Oh, how much we have lost.

Another store we would go to, which did not smell so nice, but had a sort of sharp, sour, pungent smell, was the fish store. My main memory of it is of the sawdust on the floor and the rows of big fish in the display case, right at my eye level, all with their unhappy turned-down mouths and wide-open, staring eyes that seemed to be silently begging me to help them escape, trying as hard as they could to *think* at me, pleading with me:

"Hey kid, get me out of here. *Please* get me out of here. This is all a huge, horrible mistake! C'mon, be a pal, get me out. *Please* help me. I'm not supposed to be *in* here,"

Nursing home codfish.

CHAPTER 4

A World of War

In May of 1940, Hitler finally made his move and attacked Holland, Belgium, and France, and Churchill was made prime minister virtually all at the same time.

The Germans swiftly advanced across the Netherlands, Belgium, and into northern France. The new method of war, called "blitzkrieg" (lightning war), was simply a new way of moving across territory fast, with tanks at the spearhead and tactical air support on call by radio to take out strong points; but nobody had ever done this before, and it was completely shocking to the older generals who had been taught different tactics when they were in school.

Another thing that totally faked out the Allies was that some forward-thinking younger German generals had convinced Hitler to approve a plan that sent a main part of their offensive through a mountainous area called the Ardennes. This territory was thought to be so difficult to maneuver in that the French had never expected an attack to come from that quarter and had not done much about building defenses in it. (Four years later, that same area was heard of again when the Battle of the Bulge was fought across it.)

An added twist was that several months previously, a German officer carrying the secret original plan for their invasion, which was to be almost a repeat of their thrust in the First World War, had crashed his airplane and the French had retrieved the plans. It could not have worked better if it had been a planned deception. The French and British amassed in the north, facing into Belgium, and the German mechanized armies came through the Ardennes behind them and raced to the sea, thus cutting the Allies off from the rest of France and their supplies. One of the leading German formations in that race across France was commanded by an officer named Erwin Rommel. We would hear much more from him later on.

After that the main thing I recall hearing my parents talking about was Dunkirk and the amazingly successful effort the British made to evacuate their army from the beaches there under constant air attack.

It seemed as if every story written about Dunkirk was accompanied by a picture of the huge black, sky-filling shroud of smoke that came from burning oil tanks and seemed to hang across the sky for the duration of the evacuation. The shroud of smoke actually did the British a great deal of good, because it hid half the targets that the Germans would have liked to bomb.

There are many differing opinions given for the astonishing success of the great evacuation: The mechanized German Army was undoubtedly in need of maintenance, and Hitler wanted to save them for the coming attack to the south to capture the rest of France. Luftwaffe Commander in Chief Hermann Goering's overbearing arrogance and ego led him to promise Hitler that his bombers could make the British Army surrender, so Hitler issued an order for the German Army to stop advancing. The soft sand soaked up a lot of the bombs' shrapnel and explosive power. There was a huge, unplanned outpouring of thousands of little privately owned ships from England to ferry troops from the beaches to larger ships waiting offshore. And, perhaps most important but unknowable, was the attitude of Hitler himself, who some historians think wanted to keep the British nation alive but ineffectual, to later be a balancing economic power for a German-owned Europe to trade with.

The amazing effort went on for over a week. Except for one day, there were ten days of unusually calm waters in the channel—an extremely rare event which some claimed indicated divine intervention. In the end, over 338,000 men had successfully gotten away, 123,000 of them French (many of whom, when they had the chance, went right back to France). Everybody talked about Dunkirk and what a magnificent success it had been for quite a while, but, as Churchill said, "wars are not won by evacuations."

The Germans then swept on through France, quickly occupying Paris and beyond. A truce was agreed upon, and the rest of France became a territory that cooperated with Germany but was not completely occupied. The Luftwaffe soon moved their airplanes to the French airfields on the coast, and air activity over the channel picked up.

Almost every day that spring, the British convoys in the channel were attacked by German bombers, and the British fighters that were trying to protect them tangled with the German fighter escorts. The air battles grew in size, and a number of correspondents, many of them American, were drawn to the coast, where they sometimes had what amounted to picnics while they lay on the grass and watched the show. Their published stories were generally filled with praise for the stubborn and courageous British, especially the Royal Air Force (RAF). The Germans, who could also read, brought up some very large railway guns to the French coast and started lobbing shells across the English Channel into the area around Dover. Picnics suddenly became a lot less popular.

During the summer, the air fighting moved inland as the Germans started trying to knock out the RAF airfields and these battles gradually became what's now known as the Battle of Britain.

At the time, this battle was considered epic, and in truth, it really was. After it was over, the British and their supporters in America saw it as a huge win, but the Germans to this day claim that they just sort of got tired of fighting a battle they didn't have much chance of winning. It is true that when the Germans arrived inland, near London, their main fighter, the Me 109, only had fuel enough for about fifteen minutes of high-speed fighting before they had to break it off and head for home. Many of them had to crash-land on the beaches and pastures of France, out of fuel.

And the RAF never seemed to run out of fighters. Among the German air crews of the time, a standard, cynical jab at their own propagandists was "Here they come again boys, the last fifty Spitfires!"

The German Army and Navy told Hitler, with good reason, that they must have air dominance before they could try to invade, and the Luftwaffe had not come anywhere near to that. And the fall storms, which can sometimes make the channel murderous, would soon arrive.

But it was actually a much closer contest than many histories would have readers believe. The British were not going to run out of airplanes, but they were indeed running short of fighter pilots, and the pilots still alive were terribly tired. Some of them had been flying as many as six missions a day. Several times it happened that a pilot would land, taxi in, park, and fall asleep in the cockpit. Exhausted pilots are not likely to survive long in air combat. The replacement pilots now coming to the fighter squadrons were pitifully young and inexperienced, some with only a few hours' flight time in the type of aircraft they were to take into battle. Some of them didn't even get a chance to unpack before they were killed.

The RAF leaders had already scraped the bottom of the barrel and realized they were in deep trouble because the Germans had hit upon their most effective tactic: destroying the British airfields.

Then it seemed as if providence intervened. The story goes that a German bomber crew got lost during a night raid and accidentally jettisoned their bombs on a suburb of London. Churchill promptly ordered a retaliatory raid on Berlin (he had probably just been waiting and hoping for a good excuse), and then ordered another raid the next night.

Berlin was not hurt—only a few RAF bombers found the city—but the insult to Hitler's pride was such that he ordered Goering to have the Luftwaffe switch their attacks to London and the RAF airfields were saved. Hitler made so many bad decisions like this during the war that, according to some accounts, the British decided against trying to assassinate him (and they probably could have), in order to let him go on helping them win the war.

The air war then gradually shifted to night bombing, and the British were somewhat baffled. They quickly created some "night fighters," but these were really just normal fighters with a few things like shields to keep the exhaust flames from ruining the pilots' night vision. As time went on, they were able to develop some purposely built night fighters and, most importantly, airborne radar sets, but in the beginning they had a terrible time trying to find the raiders at night.

So the British cities burned.

London of course, caught most of it, but many others, particularly Coventry, also suffered appalling damage. Hitler made up a new word, "Coventrated," for that kind of near-total obliteration of a city by firebombing.

"Give it 'em back!" the bombed-out people used to shout at Churchill when he toured the ruins. "Give it 'em back!" And of course, when he could, he did.

Tenfold.

CHAPTER 5

Radio Excitements and the Lamplighter

Since I was in kindergarten, I wasn't very aware of what was going on in the outside world during these years. The war was in all the newspapers and magazines, though; you couldn't escape it. Forever printed in my memory is a picture in the magazine section of the Sunday paper of a German airplane, a Messerschmitt 110, flying over the English Channel. The cliffs of Dover were just beyond it and seemed very close. I was astonished at how narrow the channel looked.

By this time, I had an old radio in my room. It had been my grandfather's, then became the family radio downstairs, then became mine when Mom got a nice big Magnavox console with a record player in it so she could listen to symphonic music. Among her many other talents, Mom had once been a concert pianist and she greatly enjoyed classical music.

Sunday afternoons were her time and we kids were *strongly* urged not to make noise. It was best to go upstairs or outside. She listened to the London Philharmonic Orchestra. That meant shortwave broadcasts from England, picked up and then rebroadcast on standard radio—WQXR no doubt. Sometimes Olive, our refugee friend from England, would listen with her.

Those broadcasts faded in and out, hissed and roared, seeming to come closer and then recede as the Kennelly-Heavyside and other ionospheric layers slowly surged and sank over the vast reaches of the North Atlantic. That was quite a sound, that shortwave fading in and out. It *sounded* like it came from far away. It could make you think of huge waves rolling across icy northern seas or crashing in giant curtains of white spray against distant headlands—or perhaps of the vastness of space. I miss it.

I miss the Kennelly-Heavyside Layer, too—the Heavyside part anyhow. We were taught about it in school, but now nobody mentions it anymore.

Where did it go? There were nights when I thought I could almost see it—that strange, mysterious layer, lying dark and *heavy* above the city lights on the horizon, with the dark sea beyond.

But now it's gone, just like running boards on the sides of cars, and locomotive steam whistles, and cider that gets tangy if you leave it outdoors on the back steps for a week or so.

At suppertime on Sundays, when we started to whine, "I'm hungry," we would be told, with a certain amount of overemphasis, that it was "Mom's night off" and that we had to "fend for ourselves." I think that my father was not entirely happy about fending for himself either, but we did it. Mom also often took pity on us and made helpful suggestions.

I remember those meals with a good deal of pleasure, for they were different. I particularly remember hot cocoa, sometimes with marshmallows on top. They weren't tiny little undernourished marshmallows either; they were full size. They got hard, too, if they'd been left open in the cupboard for a while. They could hurt a lot if you got into a marshmallow fight with your brother and he got you. That was fun, too, because they sometimes made a little puff of white powdered sugar smoke when they hit and left a round white mark on your target—like explosive shells. This activity was not at all favored by management.

Sometimes we were able to make sandwiches of cold roast beef left over from midday dinner, but more often it would just be plain buttered toast with sugar and cinnamon sprinkled on it. What I really liked was, once in a long while, we'd have cold popovers left over from breakfast.

I make popovers myself now, but not often enough. I wish I would. But they were better when Mom made them. Real butter and real milk and heavy, black, cast-iron popover pans make a difference, I suppose.

I wonder how many people today know what a lamplighter is, or was. I guess it now sounds a bit like something mythological, but we really had one.

Our streetlights at the time, before the war and I think for some years into it, were gas lamps. They were only about twelve feet high and had a somewhat Victorian look. They had an opaque white glass enclosure on top that diffused the light of the gas flame and had to be lifted up to light the flame. That was the job of the lamplighter.

The lamplighter would quietly arrive in his strange little truck after the sun had gone down and it was getting gloomy. Outside my window I would hear a few creaking and clinking noises—his truck seemed to have things hanging from it—and I would sometimes get out of my bed to look out the window and watch. I never did get a clear look at him; it was always getting dark when he arrived and there were some trees or bushes in the way.

There were some times when I thought I saw a companion with him, a son perhaps, learning the trade or just along for the ride. The lamplighter appeared to be a short, burly figure, in my imagination sort of ape-like. He would putter around, get a small ladder off his truck, climb up it, fiddle around, and a glare of light would suddenly appear. He seemed to adjust it a little. Then he would climb down, put the ladder back, get back in his truck, and with some small clinking noises, roll away down the street. The whole performance was nearly soundless, thus weird. He never seemed to start the little truck's engine, but then, why would he? The street was all gently downhill, he only had to go about a hundred feet to the next streetlight, and gas, after all, cost money.

At that time maybe as much as fourteen cents per gallon.

But I did have a vague feeling of nervousness about him. He seemed to be a little stealthy, and I had been sternly warned not to look out the window at him. I had the feeling that if he saw me, he might "get" me. Now I realize that it was just because I was supposed to be in bed, trying futilely to go to sleep.

I think that kids were sent to bed earlier then than is customary now. I remember all too well lying in my bed in the summer, listening to a thousand crickets loudly creaking in the field outside my window while it was still broad daylight, thinking that it was impossible to just "go to sleep," that there must be some special trick to it that I simply could not learn. In winter it was a little better, because it was dark, but I would still be wide awake when sent to bed and ordered to go to sleep and not to listen to my radio.

It usually seemed far, far too unfairly early to me, so of course, I cheated and did listen. But I had to be very careful. I had to keep the volume way, way down. I kept that volume down so low that I myself could barely hear it a foot away! I know my father couldn't hear it through the closed door, for I heard him come stealthily up and listen at my door several times, and I don't think he ever heard a thing. Sometimes I would wake up in the morning and be astonished to find my radio still on.

I kept on stubbornly listening, night after night, because I was hoping to hear something again that was as exciting as a program I had accidentally stumbled across on one of the first nights I ever tried it.

The reporter was up on a rooftop in London and was describing an air raid while it was actually happening! There were bombs: now and then you'd hear one come down and every so often you'd hear an airplane go over, but those sounds were not particularly impressive. They didn't sound like they did on *Captain Midnight*, for instance, where the airplanes sounded powerful and

the bombs all whistled piercingly. But what did amaze me was the sound of the anti-aircraft fire. It was endless! For a while I could not comprehend what I was hearing. It was a rolling continuum of explosions that never stopped. It just rolled on and on and on—
BumBumBoomToomBungBungBoomPOWPOWboomboompoompow
—in the background, like the sound of giant steam locomotive going somewhere. I was truly amazed—that was a *lot* of guns! It was very exciting.

Well, it turns out that I had by blind dumb luck stumbled across a broadcast that is now famous. The reporter was Edward R. Murrow, and he was up on the roof of the London Post Office building. It was really a pretty gutsy piece of work. Steel helmet or not, hot pieces of exploded AA shells falling from ten thousand feet will hurt any part of you that isn't under the helmet, a *lot*.

Just like me, the Londoners were evidently impressed and comforted by the continuous rolling cacophony of all those guns—they were not to find out until much later that a lot of the shells never reached the altitude of the bombers. Many of the guns were old and obsolete and had been brought in at Mr. Churchill's behest to bang away at the sky and make the people feel better. It certainly *sounded* impressive!

I don't know whether or not I was hearing the original broadcast, but the times and the year work out about right, so I think I was. He also probably did it more than once. Hearing that broadcast was a magical experience for a six-year-old, and I listened in vain night after night for something more along those lines, but I never again heard anything so exciting.

In November 1940 the British pulled off a somewhat amazing coup on the Italian fleet anchored at Taranto, a harbor on the inside of the heel of Italy. Using only a few of their old Swordfish torpedo planes, they attacked at night and disabled or sank three Italian battleships. The Italian fleet in the Mediterranean was, in one stroke, almost removed as a threat to the British.

On the other side of the world, some planners in the Japanese Navy took a keen interest in the event.

1941

CHAPTER 6

Gold and the Harbor of Pearls

In England there had been no invasion, and the daily bombings had gradually morphed into the "blitz," the nighttime bombing, mostly of London, that went on almost every night, all during the winter of 1940 and through the spring of '41.

But the British only seemed to get tougher. That was the face they and their Ministry of Information presented to the world, anyway. In reality, some were getting really, really, terribly, achingly tired of being bombed every night. Their neighborhoods had been turned to rubble; the winter winds were getting colder; there was no glass to replace a million windows that had been blown out; and sleeping in the subways (tightly packed together like sardines) was becoming more and more unpleasant. Everyone was tired. There were even some riots against the government for its failure to provide adequate air-raid shelters. Early on, the bombs seemed to be falling only on the poor people of the "East End," not the rich people in the west—which was really only a matter of who was closest to the German airfields.

Hitler finally got fed up with bombing England. He probably felt like he had given the tactic of bombing a civilian population into submission a good try (and he certainly had), but it hadn't worked. The British Army was no threat to him and would not be for a long time. The British night fighters were beginning to be able to find and knock down a few German bombers every night, but that was the only problem the RAF managed to pose Hitler. At that time the RAF bombers' night navigation was so bad that they could hardly get half their bombs within five miles of their targets. Sometimes the Germans couldn't even tell what the intended target had been!

So in the summer of '41, Hitler, after six weeks of sideshows in Yugoslavia and Greece (lost time that in the end may have cost him the war), turned on

31

Russia, which he had been wanting to do all along. His armies swept across that country with amazing speed, capturing and wiping out whole armies of Russians, one after another. The conquest had been swift, but Russia is vast, and after a while it seemed that the Germans might be getting a little tired.

Then came fall, and with fall came the rain, and what few roads there were turned to deep gullies of mud. The Germans had huge problems moving their vehicles in the mud until it got colder and the mud froze. But that only helped for a little while, because then it got a *lot* colder.

Then we started to hear that the Germans might have made a mistake—a BIG mistake. Incredibly, they didn't have any cold-weather gear, and they weren't going to get any for a long time. They were trying to fight a war in summer uniforms and tight boots at twenty below zero. Many of them froze to death and far more of them got frostbite. These were terrible conditions to attempt to continue an offensive in, but on Hitler's order, some did. One small detachment actually got to a point where they could see the spires of the Kremlin twelve miles away.

But that was as far as they ever got.

There was one time, it must have been in early 1941, when two visitors came to the house, both slender young men, both dressed in light powder-blue suits. I realize now that those must have been RAF uniforms. It may have been on a Sunday, as they had come to visit and to eat dinner. They were in America as part of a goodwill mission to make speeches and drum up American support for the war against Hitler. I think they had been part of a group that gave talks downtown somewhere, perhaps at our school auditorium, and my mother had snagged them.

Mom was very much on the side of the British. My father was too, but he was quieter about it. We should remember that this was a time when America was still at peace and the public was quite divided on the idea of getting involved in the war in Europe. (The Japanese were a bothersome itch in the Far East, but were not taken seriously.) We should also remember that at this time the RAF, especially the pilots, were *huge* heroes to many people in the United States, for they were the only military organization in the world that had so far been able to stand up to Hitler and, in a hard-fought cliff-hanger of a battle, beat him back.

About all I remember about the two RAF men is that they were friendly. During their visit my mother was greatly taken with the beauty of some badges they wore, which were in the shape of a wreath about two inches wide with the letters "RAF" inside the wreath. (The British do make some fine looking badges and insignias. I'm sad to say, they make many of our own Air

Force's badges look like something obtained through a process involving Wheaties box tops.)

My father got one of the men to lend him one of his badges long enough to make an impression of it in some clay. Then he later took the mold to a dentist friend to help him get it cast in dental gold. A really lovely pin resulted, which my mother wore with pride for many years. It was not only good looking and unique, it also showed the world where her sympathies lay. It had lost a lot of detail in the amateur casting process, but it looked massive and solid, and it was. It was undoubtedly worth even more than its weight in gold because (I have been told) the dental gold had some platinum mixed in. I can still see my mother, with the white collar of her blouse showing at her throat and the gold badge gleaming proudly on her navy blue blazer, looking like a million dollars, about to go out to some social event.

The badge finally disappeared in a house robbery, and I knew that, of all the things she'd lost, she missed that pin just about the worst.

Well, as fate would have it, I went to a military collectables show years later and there, sitting in a case along with a lot of other badges, was a badge just like the parent of the one stolen from my mother. It was not gold—I suppose it was bronze—and though it had a lot of detail in it that mother's didn't, the metal was thin and light, as if it had been stamped out along with hundreds of thousands of others.

As it had been. It was an "Other Ranks Badge" ("other ranks" being everyone in the RAF who is not an officer). It was about as rare as the buttons on their blouses. Be that as it may, the RAF badge still looked good. So I bought it, had it gold-plated, and gave it to Mom on her birthday. It was not as heavy and royal looking as the original, but she liked it.

I know nothing more about the two RAF men. I presume they went back to England and back to war.

I hope they made it.

In school, in *My Weekly Reader*, we read about the Boeing "Stratoliner," the first big four-engine passenger plane to be pressurized and to fly so high that it was above most turbulence. I was fascinated by the story and the odd look of the big airplane and never forgot about it. The Stratoliners were later painted olive drab and went to war as cargo planes. If you look at the wing and tail design, you can see a direct relationship to the famous B-17 Flying Fortress.

To my great delight, the only one that still can fly, stripped of its olive drab paint, now shines in gleaming mirror-like glory in the Aerospace Museum annex near Dulles airport, and I, seventy years after first reading about it, actually got to touch it!

Another thing *My Weekly Reader* told us about in first grade was how a big oil pipeline called "The Big Inch" was being built from somewhere down south, maybe Texas, all the way up to somewhere on the east coast, and how the amount of oil in the world was getting to be less and less and how it was going to run out soon.

From that day on, the oil has always been about to run out, but it never does.

Maybe it would be a good thing if it finally did.

Late in 1941 a strange phrase, "Nomura and Kurusu," seemed to come up in the grown-ups' talk a lot. I didn't know what it meant. It impressed me because it sounded so strange.

Then came December 7, 1941, and some big changes. I suppose almost everyone who was alive then can remember where they were when they heard about the Japanese attack on Pearl Harbor. I was lying on the living room floor, where I had most likely been reading the Sunday comics (the "funny papers"). Probably a friend of my parents had called and told us to turn on the radio. I remember lying there, listening to a very excited announcer. I can still see the rug.

1942

Chapter 7

Winter and the Quarry

Now things started to change.

For one thing, at school, in Mrs. Fiero's second grade classroom, I suddenly had a big problem with the year. The year had changed, and I had to learn to make a big numeral "2" on the blackboard instead of the "1" that I had gotten comfortable with in 1941. When it was your turn, you see, you got to write in big chalk letters on the blackboard what the day and the current date were. To be able to write it without any mistakes was a big deal. I had a lot of trouble adjusting to that "2." I felt betrayed.

So I practiced it, and the next time it was my turn, I turned out a beautiful, perfect "1942." When you got the whole thing right, you were authorized to write your name on the blackboard with the words "no help" after it.

I proudly wrote, "NO HALP."

I can still feel the shame.

We also stood to attention beside our desks every morning and, holding our hands over our hearts, recited the pledge of allegiance to the flag. We were taught quite a lot about the flag and how to treat it. It can be interesting at times to realize how lasting some of that training was.

One evening recently, while taking down my flag, I accidentally dropped it. An uneasy feeling of dread came over me and I hunched my shoulders, half expecting a big ominous figure wearing a red white and blue striped suit and white beard to step out of the shadows and roar his disapproval at me. I guiltily hoped that no one had seen me.

Some of those early lessons really stuck.

I think that during the war years the winters were unusually cold. Milk came in glass bottles and was left at the back door in the mornings by a delivery man who drove a little, boxlike truck with open doors. The sign on it read, *Alderney Dairy*. For some reason I was convinced that their milk was much better than milk from Borden's, who delivered their milk from an almost identical truck. Some mornings it was so cold that the cream, which separated naturally from the milk and always floated at the top of the bottle, would have frozen and expanded right up out of the bottles in strange-looking, curled-over cylinders, like semi-melted thick, white candles, with the milk bottle caps at the ends.

Normally, from unfrozen bottles, Mom would pour off the cream and put it in a small pewter cream pitcher that sat on the table for coffee.

Glass bottles caused some other problems, too, because they could be slippery. About once a year, one would get away from Mom (who was a fast mover), and there would be a blood-curdling shriek ("EEYEEeeeyooOOOP!"), which you could hear all over the house, then a shattering crash, and the kitchen floor would be covered with little half-inch pieces of glass and, of course, a quart of milk. Milk, like blood, goes a long way when it's spread around.

But the amazing thing, which everybody noticed and remarked upon, was that in the horrified, stunned silence after the scream and crash, the back doorbell would still be softly singing, quietly resonating like a tuning fork with Mom's horrified shriek.

I don't know if the cold the Germans were facing in Russia was part of a phenomenon that extended to the whole northern hemisphere or not, but there were times when there were great ice-flows down the face of the cliffs behind our house and huge, foot-thick icicles, ten or more feet long, hanging from ledges in the quarry. You could get killed if you were standing under one when it fell. (Of course, once in a while, I did briefly stand under them, for the thrill of it.) Sometimes, when a high wind was blowing, I would stand in the road, where the wind squeezed through the roadcut, and lean against it at a forty-five–degree angle. That worked even better if I opened my coat up and held it open like a sail, but then things would get pretty chilly. Another drawback was that sometimes the wind would suddenly die, and without warning Maria would drop me abruptly on the road.

I don't know if the Hudson River ever froze solid, but I certainly did see it thickly filled with great broken chunks of ice as big as desks and cars, all jumbled up against each other for as far as the eye could see. They were brown at the bottom.

The family photo albums show pictures of some pretty deep snows, too. I remember wading in it up to my chest, but I was probably only about three or four feet tall then.

I suppose it is possible that we caught a little extra snow because of where we lived. My father had picked his location well. The town is shaped like a rectangle and lies with its long axis running north-south, sloping up from the east toward its western boundary, which runs along the top of a long ridge called the first Watchung "mountain." The second Watchung is another ripple in the land a few miles west. "Watchung," I have been told, is a Lenni-Lenape Indian word which means something like "good place to spend winter."

Sort of like Miami or Naples, right?

"Mountain" is in quotes because anyone from Idaho or Colorado would laugh loud and long, but still, the Watchungs are the first high ground you come to west of Hoboken. And, having several times been up there around two in the morning, when it was eighteen degrees with a pretty stiff wind blowing, I can tell you that the top of the first Watchung is not always like Miami or Naples either.

My father had found a plot of land to build on that was right at the very western edge of town and probably at about the highest point, too. Some years later, a white line was painted across the street (I don't know why) that showed exactly where the boundary was. It was only a few feet up the road from our driveway. Beyond that, the road became "Old Quarry Road," which tells you a little about what came next. The quarry was just beyond our back yard and had been abandoned for at least fifty years. What they quarried there was an unusually hard and dense type of basalt called "traprock," used for making gravel and concrete. Another thick layer of the same rock slants upward beneath North Jersey and lies exposed along the western edge of the Hudson River. That's called the Palisades.

The only signs that the quarry had ever been worked were the large holes, about an inch wide and intended for dynamite sticks, that were bored into many of the piano-sized boulders lying on the quarry floor. On top of the north cliff there was a circular concrete platform about three feet high and twenty feet in diameter that had been the base for a large water tank. The quarry floor was almost flat, but the south side would hold about a foot of water if it had rained for a day or two.

When it filled, Jackie, my friend Nancy's older brother, liked to get up on top of the south cliff with me and throw the biggest rocks we could find into the water below. He called the big boulders on the quarry floor "The Philippines" (which were much in the news in early 1942) and liked to play like we were bombing them. The bigger the missile, the bigger the splash, so naturally we searched for the biggest rocks we could find. There was once a fair selection of rocks up there, but after about ten years, there were no rocks to be found within several hundred feet of the edge in any direction. The ground had been picked clean, for we were far from being the only kids who went up there.

In those days, when the quarry had water in it, there would often be a small waterfall coming down from a rock outcrop about fifteen feet above our backyard. It drained across the side yard and down a vacant lot to the street. Mom liked that waterfall. She liked to look out the window and see it while doing the dishes. Later, after something had been done up in the quarry that made it stop flowing, she missed it.

In later years, I tried to recreate it for her by constructing a concrete catch-basin with a submersible pump and hose leading up to where the waterfall had been, but it was not entirely successful. After three expensive pumps had burned out because of absentminded activations with no water in the sump, a big piece of tape appeared over the switch that said, "DON'T TURN ON."

Then, more years later, the big piece of sandstone—as big as a Volkswagon beetle—where the waterfall came from, itself fell onto the concrete basin (at night, fortunately), totally erasing all evidence of my efforts. It lies there today, a large, angular, reddish-brown monster, half hidden by some rhododendrons that I think Mom may have planted to try to hide it. Beneath it somewhere lie some pieces of concrete and the crushed remains of what was once a submersible pump.

I somewhat guiltily suspect that water seeping down behind the rock had periodically frozen and expanded and hastened the fall of that boulder by several centuries.

Don't tell Mom.

Standing at the middle of the quarry, you were at the center of a circle perhaps two hundred yards in diameter, but it seemed bigger. It seemed like a hidden world in which you were surrounded by vertical cliffs about eighty feet high, which then became lower as they narrowed down to a cut for the road in the west. The road went right through the quarry's middle. The area was wide open on the east.

I always just accepted the quarry as part of my life. It was just there. It was where I lived. Later in life, as I have learned a little more about geology, I have realized some of its unusual features. I think that the thick layer of dense, igneous rock that formed the cliffs behind our house is somewhat rare and that it and the Palisades along the Hudson River may be about the only two places where it surfaces.

But beneath that, exposed and forming the twenty-foot-high back wall of our back yard, there was a layer of red sandstone that went down who knows how deep. That sandstone is ancient. There are some fossils in the rocks above it, but none in the sandstone. Not of animals or plants anyhow.

What is there, somewhere, is a layer of fossilized raindrops. I have a thin piece about two inches square, but at the time I didn't think they were very interesting at all. I now think those are pretty rare and wish I had done some serious excavating to find the layer containing them. Somewhere in all those centuries of red mud being laid down—behind our garage, there was the exposed edge of a stack about ten feet deep, a thousand crumbly layers, each one about a sixteenth of an inch thick—lies hidden a magic stratum covered with those incredibly ancient pockmarks.

Grandpa had taught me a little geology (and generated an interest that has lasted all my life). It was amazing to realize that those raindrops fell millions and millions of years before there were any people, perhaps millions of years before there were even any land animals at all. And still, the simple mechanics of rainfall and fossilizing worked just like they do now, except that perhaps what was falling would not have tasted quite the same as what we now call rain.

On the other hand, who knows? There may have been all sorts of things that arose and then disappeared in ancient forgotten times and have left no trace (perhaps intentionally).

Or maybe fossils are just a trick.

I would sit sometimes behind the garage, doped off in the summer sun, surrounded by a talus slope of crumbled sandstone bits, and think that where I was sitting could have once been the shore of some prehistoric beach, drowned in a huge, unimaginable pile of ancient years, so far back that the land was flat and barren, perhaps even without plants.

The nights would have been amazing, though. Incredibly clear air, with perhaps many more bright stars and comets wheeling overhead than we now see, but with none of the familiar constellations and a much bigger and brighter moon. In the daytime there would be just an amazingly bright, dark-blue, empty sky, empty ocean, and a vast deserted beach. Nothing moving anywhere but the far, far-away waves, hard to see because the beach, owing to the much greater tides, was so wide.

That would have been lonely.

There were gravels of other varieties besides traprock in the quarry, too. Above the sandstone layer there were, here and there, outcrops of some kind of rock that looked old and rotten. It had been bubbly lava, and was now crumbly, filled with voids and cracks, and had all sorts of things imbedded in it. There were definitely fossils here, but I never found anything but what looked like tiny little scallop shells about half an inch long. There were also what looked like little starbursts of orange feldspar and quartz. There was one amazing find I dug out, completely by accident, that looked like a rock about the size of a tennis ball. I cracked it open with a hammer and was amazed to see it fall in two halves of what looked like a big, solid piece of dark agate. I kept it and finally, many years later, took it to a gem shop to see if it could be cut and polished smoothly, but when they tried to cut it, they found they couldn't do it; it had too many fractures in it. They did polish it for me, as best they could. They said they thought it was not agate, but was probably smoky quartz. I'm not convinced. It looks intriguingly mysterious, anyhow, and I still have it.

Aside from knowing where to find fossils and quartz and feldspar, I also knew about a place where there were real semi-precious stones. We called it the "Amethyst Mine." There was a cut in the quarry rocks that narrowed down to a small crevice about a foot wide, and at the bottom, in the dark greenish rock, was a vein of color about an inch wide, white at the sides and purple in the middle, which was the amethyst. Each crystal was only about a quarter of an inch across, but with careful extraction you could get some flat pieces a couple of inches wide, solidly covered with crystals. For a little kid it was a lot like how it must feel to prospect for and find gold.

Very few people knew about this place and I think a lot fewer do now. We thought of it as a family secret.

There was a state teachers college a few miles to the north of us, and I suspect that for many years there may have been a geology professor up there who told his classes about the quarry and urged them to get their hammers and chisels and get up there on weekends to do some prospecting. He already knew what I was to find out: there was a whole lot of interesting stuff to be dug up in that quarry.

For many years, on weekends with good weather, the air was always filled with the *dink dink, dink, dink* of a few prospectors, students I suppose, chipping away with their hammers at the rocks. They were rarely in the places where the good stuff was.

And any time I hear that sound it takes me back.

Chapter 8

Neighbors and Winter Nights

Across the street from us, on the curve in the road, was the McKinneys' house. Mrs. McKinney was an older lady who lived with and took care of her brother, who was not in good health. They were both very pale. Their big old house had been the last one on the street for many years, and they had not been at all pleased when my father built our house across the street from them.

But Mother, an adept amateur psychologist, had sent me across the street with an empty measuring cup to ask if we could borrow some sugar. I was two or three years old at the time and evidently irresistible, because it worked. There was peace between neighbors from then on. My father would go downtown on Sunday mornings to get some ice cream and two Sunday papers, then I was detailed to take one of them, the McKinneys' paper, across to them.

Mrs. McKinney had a little dog named "Effie." In dog years, Effie seemed to be about the same age as the McKinneys and was spoken to as if she were a willful child. Sometimes when their front door was open, Effie would make a break for it. Then, outside my window I would hear a slow-motion parade going up the street. Neither the little dog nor Mrs. McKinney could walk very fast, but Effie's little legs would go just fast enough to keep her ahead and out of reach. Listening to their passage could be fun:

"Effie, come back here."

"Young lady, you come right back here this minute."

"Do you want me to get a stick?"

"Effie, I've had just about enough of this."

"Do you want me to take steps?"

"I'm going to get a stick then."

"Alright, I'm going to have to take steps."

This last had a legalistic ring to it. I wondered if Effie was going to hear from a lawyer.

I don't know what would happen next. I suppose Effie finally made it to the quarry and found out it wasn't the Promised Land after all. They were both probably pretty winded by that time, so I guess the fugitive was apprehended and brought back to endure a stern talking-to.

These little episodes were very entertaining.

During the war it came to Mrs. McKinney that she could outwit the ration board by keeping some chickens. She also had a rooster, which could occasionally be irritating in the mornings, but I think he may have irritated the McKinneys too, because he didn't last.

This was all a great problem for my father. He had been the town planner and was painfully aware of the zoning laws, one of which stipulated that no farm animals could be kept in zoned residential areas. He was in a moral quandary, knowing that blowing the whistle on Mrs. McKinney would ruin the more or less friendly relations between the two families.

Finally some sort of arrangement was made and in return for silence on the matter we got a small, periodic supply of free eggs for the rest of the war.

The cliffs were a natural place to learn how to climb, and we did a lot of it.

Our favorite route to the top of the cliffs was a vertical climb of about sixty feet. My brother and I timed each other and found we could do it in seven seconds. There was no point in timing the descent—it was just a kind of controlled free-fall drop, slowed some by a few hand and foot grabs, and it took about two seconds.

My friends and I would sometimes play a game called "cliff tag." This was a game that would have surely sent any parent who witnessed it into nervous fits and would have led to being instantly forbidden from doing it any more. Well, maybe not instantly, for fear of startling the players, who were stuck on the vertical face of the cliff in the most inaccessible places they could find, places so dangerous to get to that he who was "it" was not able or was afraid to climb close enough to them to tag them. Since it was my "territory," I took great personal pride in being able to outclimb anyone else. I well remember clinging with the fingertips of my right hand to a half-inch little shelf and the edge of my left shoe (much stiffer than the athletic shoes kids mostly wear now) wedged into another little half-inch shelf, supported by nothing else and arching my body in slow motion away from the stretching hand of the guy who was "it," all while about thirty feet above the quarry floor. That's about the most dangerous physical thing I've ever done . . . though there have been some other times in my life when only luck or some sort of unseen spirit guardian could have explained my survival.

There was a good view from on top of the cliff. All of north Jersey was spread out at our feet and the city was a blue picket fence on the horizon. At night there was an uncountable number of little twinkling lights, a blanket of them spread across the land from as far north as you could see to just as far south, beyond Newark and Staten Island.

In the winter mornings I would awake to a far-away, high, wailing sound coming from the hot air register in my room, which was closed, but did let a little of the air get by. It could be that my father had gone downstairs and turned up the thermostat, or maybe it came on by itself—I never thought about it. My outlet was always closed because I liked the cold air and always slept with my window slightly open.

I could see thousands, no, millions, of lights all the way out to the horizon from there. A lot of the lights were in Newark. Newark is not thought to be a particularly charming place, but seeing it from a distance as I did, it was a magical pile of lights out there on the horizon.

There were a few times when I awoke, thoroughly chilled, and realized that I was lying with my legs still in the bed and my upper body on the windowsill with the pillow under me where I had lain to get a better view.

Sometimes I saw some startling things out that window. One night I awoke, I don't know why, to see several amazingly bright, *big* searchlight beams shining up into the sky from somewhere very close. They looked almost violet around their edges, and there were at least two of them, maybe three. I was astonished. One of them seemed to be coming from a place just down our street! Yet I had heard nothing, and the world outside was completely silent. That was the weird part: there were no airplanes; there was no sound at all.

I was quite sure that I would have known about it had there been any construction of anti-aircraft batteries going on in our neighborhood, but I had heard of nothing.

The lights waved around in the sky for a while, then one came down and pointed horizontally toward the east, where New York was. It was a soundless performance and all very mysterious. After a while, the lights went out and I eventually went back to sleep . . . wondering.

Sometime later—seems to me it was weeks later, but it must have been related to what I had seen that night—I was riding in the car with my mother and I saw a large, olive-drab truck, and a trailer with a big searchlight mounted on it, parked at the side of the road right below ours. The big box on the truck must have been the generator. I don't remember ever hearing anybody say anything about it, but it must have been a test of some kind of the air defenses in the area around New York. What they thought we might be attacked by is a mystery. Aircraft carriers perhaps, but the Germans had none. Maybe airplanes launched from submarines. I guess there was probably some hysteria about how technologically capable the enemy had proven to be and that maybe they could come up with some sort of gigantic long-range bomber, but that turned out to be a needless worry.

Late in the war, just to prove they could do it, they actually did build one such aircraft, and it did manage to get all the way across the ocean to within about ten miles of New York, but then they just turned around and trundled on back. They didn't bring any bombs with them, either.

In February of 1942 a wonderful new scheme was announced to help us win the war even sooner: DOUBLE wartime saving time!

This meant you had to set your clock two hours ahead when you converted to daylight saving time, instead of one . . . at least I *think* that was how it was supposed to work. I remember a lot of quite animated discussion about it at the dinner table. But my father overruled everybody. I was told I would have to get up an hour early, and an alarm clock was specially set. Whatever we were supposed to do, my father got it wrong. He was going to take me to school and drop me off on his way to work. As I remember, it was all very confused, getting up an hour early and getting ready and all that, and I felt sort of sick. But finally we took off and went down to the school a mile away. The school was deserted, but my father told me to get out and wait and that someone would open the doors pretty soon.

So I got out, he drove off, and there I waited. And waited. And waited. There was nobody else around. Nothing was happening. Nothing. It was dead quiet. I tried some doors but they were all locked. Finally, I sat down on the steps. It was cold and dark. Real dark. Really, really dark. Then my butt got cold on the concrete. I stood up again. Then I started to think I saw something moving in the gloom among the bicycle racks on the other side of the driveway. It had to be a German soldier! Or maybe sailors landed from a submarine! I sat there nervously checking the bicycle shed for what seemed like a *long* time, but eventually someone inside the school unlocked the door and I was able to go in.

We had been an hour too early. Daylight saving time doesn't start in February.

I don't remember what my father may have had to say about the episode that evening, nor did I hear what comments my mother may have made, but we never repeated the exercise.

I don't think that double wartime saving time was very popular. I imagine that a lot of other people were also confused.

Somewhere around this time a big French ocean liner, the *Normandie*, caught fire and burned at her pier in New York. The ship was being converted to serve as a troop ship and the story put out was that some careless welding had ignited some waste rags and set the ship on fire. There was also a lot of talk about sabotage for a while, but in the end it was declared an accident. It probably was sabotage, but maybe not by Nazis.

I've seen a sort of documentary TV program which stated that the Mob was somehow involved in the fire and that some sort of a deal was then worked out between Mob kingpin Lucky Luciano (who was in jail serving a fifty-year sentence at the time) and the FBI, which resulted in there never being any espionage or sabotage on the docks for the rest of the war. Lucky Luciano was soon moved to a much nicer, friendlier jail, and later, after a decent waiting period of several years had passed, Mr. Luciano was paroled because he had been such a good boy.

After he got out, he naturally went right back to being a bad boy again.

I had been a collector of pictures of big ships for several years and the *Normandie* had been one of the three biggest ones that worked the North Atlantic. The other two were the *Queen Mary* and the *Queen Elizabeth*. I had pictures of them all, clipped from magazines. Later I got a picture of the *Normandie* lying on its side in the water at its dock. It seems they pumped it so full of water to put the fire out that it capsized. It looked pretty sad and useless, lying there on its side like an enormous beached whale.

It was never used as a troopship. Maybe they thought it would just be too much trouble. Eventually it was sold for scrap.

CHAPTER 9

Air Raids, Real and Imagined

In the spring of 1942, the famous Doolittle Raid on Japan took place. I remember a lot of people talking about *that* for a while. It made everybody feel pretty good. It showed that we could hit back and quite cleverly, too. It was a nice piece of payback for Pearl Harbor. The president was very cagey about where the bombers had come from, too; he told the press that they came from Shangri-La (a mythical kingdom in the Himalayas) at first, which struck some people as devilishly clever.

The raid was a real tonic and had been badly needed—up until then in the Pacific, we and the British (and the Australians and the Dutch) just hadn't seemed to be able to do anything right. Everything went wrong and the "little yellow men" had just kicked our butts all over the place. This was doubly shocking because up until then, it had been fashionable for many uninformed Caucasian people to look down upon the Japanese with mild contempt.

On the west coast there was a lot of worry that the Japanese, since they were doing so well, might actually invade. Finally, in February, hysteria won out and an event now sardonically called "The Battle of Los Angeles" took place. Nobody knows what actually set it off—it may have been some poor weenie in a civilian plane—but after someone started firing into the sky at something, everybody else who could squeeze a trigger joined in. It made everybody feel better.

In the end thousands and thousands of anti-aircraft shells and bullets of all sizes had been fired off, some of which, improperly fused, came right back down and landed in the city, which, of course, was taken as actual proof of bombing.

There was one time several months later when a real attack actually did occur, but it was not exactly earthshaking. A Japanese submarine surfaced near a small town north of Santa Barbara where there was a small oil refinery and pumped a few shells in the refinery's direction from the sub's deck gun. Very little damage was done.

It is possible that the choice of that particular target may have been due to an old grudge held by the submarine's captain. Seems that before the war he had been a guest of the United States on some sort of liaison tour and, while touring that oil refinery, had stumbled and sat down heavily on a cactus, which caused much merriment on the part of his American Naval hosts and great embarrassment to him. So when war had been declared and he had the chance, he surfaced his sub and let fly with a few shells, thus avenging his loss of face.

All of America was hugely outraged and instantly united by the perceived treachery of the Japanese. Their attack on Pearl Harbor had come while their ambassadors Nomura and Kurusu (aha!) were actually in the process of talking peace in Washington. There had been no formal declaration of war before the attack (I guess right about then was when the old formal, polite way of commencing a war went out the window, probably forever).

The outrage lasted for a long time and blended quickly into hate and bloodlust. When the stories of horrible atrocities began to filter back from the men fighting in the Pacific, the hatred became even worse. Now they were no longer called "Japanese"; now they were called "Japs."

But it seems to me that where I was, people were more worried about the Germans. Hitler had declared war on us only a few days after the Japs did, which made an ongoing undeclared naval war in the North Atlantic suddenly "legal." (Their submarines had been firing torpedoes at our ships, and we had been depth charging them, for months. At the end of October, one of our destroyers, the *Reuben James*, had been sunk with all hands.) On the east coast the Germans were certainly a lot closer to us, and within a few weeks after the war started, their submarines, right offshore, started sinking our ships at a horrifying rate.

The story of how we dealt with, or failed to deal with, the sinkings for the first half-year is a sorry tale of stupidity, pride, and amateurishness. We had nowhere near the number of destroyers and other small ships that we needed to protect the merchant ships along the east coast. Worse yet, we refused to follow the much more effective convoying method that the British had followed for many years, largely because Admiral King thoroughly disliked the British and wanted no part of taking their advice. Not only that, but the cities along the east coast at first stubbornly refused to observe government blackout requests (because "it would ruin the tourist season"), and so the ships sailed along the coast at night, silhouetted against the bright sky glow of the cities on the horizon.

So a shameful number of them got sunk. Seventy in the Atlantic during February alone.

Even ten years later down at the shore, if there had been a storm or unusually high tide, where the beach had been cut away you could still see the thin layers of black about a sixteenth of an inch thick, alternating with clean layers of sand, one above the other like tree rings, sometimes as many as eight or ten, each one recording an exploded, burned, and sunken tanker.

The stuff balled up in little lumps the size of acorns and Ping-Pong balls too. Sometimes those "tar balls" were all over the beach, and it was almost inevitable that you'd get some on your feet, which, if you later walked on some mother's clean rug, could lead to loud expressions of extreme displeasure and even banishment.

All of this happening right on our doorstep as it were, with deep layers of stinking black oil (and it *did* stink) from sunken tankers puddling on the beaches and the fires of torpedoed ships frequently visible on the horizon at night, got people pretty excited, as you might imagine. All sorts of rumors and tall tales started to circulate.

Sometimes the excitement would creep all the way up to where we lived. There was one time—it had to be in the spring of '42 because we weren't wearing winter coats—sometime in midmorning, when the school fire alarm suddenly went off: *BLANG! BLANG! BLANG! BLANG!* Now, *there* was a sound that would almost stop your heart and send you about two feet up in the air! "Alarm bell" is right. It was extremely alarming!

Then you would find your partner. (We all had to have partners. Mine was Nancy. She was the only other kid my age who lived anywhere near our house, so of course we were friends and partners.) Two by two, with the alarm still sounding—*BLANG! BLANG! BLANG! BLANG!*—and the teacher trying to tell us what to do, we'd hold hands and file in a more or less orderly manner out of the room. But this time we didn't go outside. We took a right instead and went down the stairs into the basement. *BLANG! BLANG! BLANG!* (I'll bet our heart rates were up around 200 beats per minute by this time.) We were told to sit in orderly rows on the floor with our backs to the wall and to be quiet. ("Hmmm . . . *this* is no ordinary fire drill . . . ") I don't know how long we were there, but it was certainly long enough to get bored and restless. ("NO TALKING!") I did hear some murmurs about an air raid, but even though I was only in second grade, I thought I knew enough about airplanes even then to consider that absurd.

Then, to my amazement, I saw one of the younger teachers run by, and she was actually crying! Tears streaming down her cheeks! I could hardly believe it. *Tears?* Adults don't cry, do they? What was there to *cry* about anyhow? Even if there *was* an air raid with real airplanes and real bombs and real explosions—why, that would be one of the neatest, most exciting, most wonderful things you could possibly imagine!

I don't know, maybe she was just scared—afraid of being raped perhaps— her mind filled full of the propaganda and rumors of those times. Maybe she had been spoken to sharply by one of the older teachers or even the *principal* . . . maybe she had even been slapped, "to snap her out of it," you know. (That helpful little custom, frequently seen in the movies of those times, was sometimes being used a little too enthusiastically by some impressionable people, especially young girls, who probably thought it was a fun thing to get away with.)

Well, after a while they got a "plan" together and sent us all home.

Now, just imagine that. Suddenly in the middle of the day, with no notice, the town fills up with little kids, all walking home alone or with a partner who lives in the same neighborhood. Little kids walking, in some cases (like ours), almost a mile home, where there might or might not be an adult. I wonder what would happen today if the school authorities pulled a stunt like that?

But it wasn't actually as bad as it might sound. There were very few cars (no gas). The town was very quiet then. Sexual predators? Well, I suppose they have always been with us, but I'd never heard of any. Of course the adults weren't about to *tell* us if there was anything like that going on, but I do have the impression that there was a lot less of it then than there is now. If any such thing were reported in the newspapers, you'd have had to read between the lines to find it. As I remember, Nance and I just walked home calmly together, not thinking much about it, just doing what we'd been told to do, kind of happy to be out of school early.

I believe what had happened was that a submarine had been sighted close to the coast, and everybody, school authorities included, had come unglued. I think that there was later a lot of unfavorable commentary about it, too, from parents who were less than pleased about having their children set adrift in the middle of the day.

I wonder what Mom thought when I appeared at that hour? I remember she was surprised, of course, and I got quizzed a bit, then she got right on the phone. Nancy's mother first, then the school, I guess. Then she reappeared with a bemused little smile and, I realize now, a contemptuous expression. Thinking back on it, I realize that's probably exactly what it was—she couldn't believe it! Mom had no patience for "weak sisters."

Those faint-hearted, lily-livered cowards at the school, even including the *principal*, had obviously panicked, sent the kids home early, and thereby ruined whatever plans she'd had—and over what? A U-boat scare?

"Well, how is a U-boat possibly going to hurt us here? We're eighteen miles from the ocean! . . . You what? *Who* told you to? The military district? Well, who are they? How can they tell the schools . . . really? Well, that's *stupid!*"

All part of the learning curve. We didn't know how to work a war yet.

CHAPTER **10**

Getting to Know the Principal

Mr. McClain, our principal, had what I thought was a genuinely chilling aspect. Now, I'm sure that he was actually a very nice person. I think, in fact, that he, in that infinitely far-off, distant, hidden dimension where the adults go to talk with each other about you, was a sort of a "friend" of my parents. I heard my mother refer to him as "Bill" once and couldn't believe my ears.

I don't think you understand. That was like it would have been if I'd heard her call the *president* "Frank"! It was enough to scramble my brains.

Anyway, in his work dealing with an endless succession of vast crowds of small, energetic, crafty monkeys, Mr. McClain had developed some really effective ways to instill awe and create discipline just by his appearance! When we had an "assembly" he had a way of standing there at the podium above the heaving, twisting, twitching, whispering, giggling mass of perhaps 400 children and tilting his noble, handsome head with high cheekbones back so that the overhead lights reflected off his steel-rimmed glasses (or were they rimless?). And you *could not see his eyes!* Just twin circles of shining light. Staring right at *you.* Scary.

Mr. McClain was tall and thin and gave me the impression that he was made of spring steel. For some reason, I had the idea that he had done something heroic during World War I. In my memory he is always dressed in a gray suit. He had wavy gray hair and his features were what one would call "chiseled." I think he looked a lot like an actor named Laurence Stone, whom we don't see much any more.

Looking back on it, I think that the way Mr. McClain tilted his head back so the lights reflected off his glasses may have just been a matter of optics. Maybe he saw better at a distance by looking under his glasses.

Whatever it was, it was effective.

Being "sent to the principal" was theoretically about one of the most serious things that could possibly happen to you. It was about like being drummed out of some foreign legion. Being stripped of your decorations one by one and having your sword broken—in front of the entire battalion.

And of course, it wasn't a *private* sentencing. You weren't taken aside and told you were going to "see the principal" in a whisper. Oh nooo . . . not hardly. It was quite the opposite: a very clear and *public* denunciation and humiliation ("Off with his head!"), which was, of course, the point. I had one friend who was so upset by it all that he wet his pants. That did get him out of a trip to the principal, as a matter of fact, but it did not spare him any embarrassment.

And then you would go, all alone, on the long walk. All alone, mulling over your crime. All alone, down the long, echoing hall toward . . . the OFFICE.

As you walked, you'd contemplate your chances of surviving the consequences if you just bolted! Out a side door, down the street . . . but what then? You knew they'd find you. Even at that age you suspected that the sight of a little kid, furtively darting from tree to tree in the middle of the day, might well attract some unwanted adult attention. And so you trudged on, filled with fear and remorse. That was the theory anyway, I guess.

In actuality, those times when it happened to me, I remember being quite baffled. "Now, what the hell is *this* all about, I wonder? I didn't do anything wrong!" is what I remember thinking mostly. (I would not have *dared* to say that out loud, by the way.)

Usually it had to do with pictures I had drawn, I think. It took me most of seventy years to almost learn this lesson: management does *not like* cartoons that make fun of it. But of course, you wouldn't draw a cartoon that didn't make fun of *something*, would you? And after all, management is usually such an easy target. Bill Mauldin would understand.

When you got to the big office, there would be some women behind the counter. They might look at you seriously, and some might look a little like they were trying not to smile (again: "Now, what the hell does *that* mean, I wonder?"), and you would have to tell them why you were there and then sit on the cold, hard bench and wait. All of which was cleverly designed to be intimidating, I suppose, but was pretty interesting really. It was something like going to the doctor. With less fear. It got you out of the classroom, anyhow.

Then you might or might not get ushered into the *really scary* inner sanctum, where Mr. McClain lived. Well it was scary the first time. After that, it was just an office. Mr. McClain might ask you why you were there. I learned early that it was a good idea to play real dumb.

"I don't know. Miss Marshall sent me to show you this drawing." I actually thought once that perhaps she wanted him to see it because it was so *good*.

He might take the drawing and look at it, then move around his desk and look out the window for a while, as if deciding my fate (I realize now that he may have just been trying to keep a straight face, or perhaps trying to think how to handle not me, but Miss Marshall—a new, young teacher who might have been having a little trouble coming down to the right rpm).

Once, after telling me not to do it again, whatever it was, he suddenly smiled and warmly asked me how my mother was! Now, that *was* a surprise. He also said to tell her he said hello. This again scrambled my brains badly. It was like having the guy who worked the guillotine ask you how you like your eggs done!

Maybe, come to think of it, it was all part of a clever plot, wherein I would get asked by my mother how come I had been talking with her friend Bill, and then the fat would be in the fire. Very clever, but it ignores the fact that little kids sometimes forget to relay messages . . . especially ones that may involve self-incrimination.

Nah, that's not it.

More likely, Mom, who at the time was probably a cute, trim, pert little redhead, had been taking a hand in social and school affairs, probably involving plantings and floral decorations, and had attracted some admiring attention.

Early in the war, a thing we did at least once was to sit or kneel in the playground, arranged in a circle around Mr. King, our gym teacher, and wait for 11 a.m. to come. This was on November 11th, Armistice Day, (so we were waiting for the eleventh hour of the eleventh day of the eleventh month, you see). At 11 a.m., the town's fire siren went off, and then we observed a minute of complete silence when we were not allowed to talk.

Armistice day had seemed pretty significant when it was originally designated, I suppose, symbolic of the ending of "The War to End All Wars" and all that. But when WWII came so soon and looked like it was going to be even worse, Armistice Day seemed to lose a lot of its importance. In addition, I think sounding the sirens in mid-morning like that, with no warning to all the people in town who had no idea it was Armistice Day and were convinced it was an air raid, turned out to be somewhat unpopular.

Mr. King will always be remembered by his gym classes for the way he always announced the end of the period. In a stentorian voice, he would command, "Alright men, pick up two rocks and go to the gate," and we would have to look for pebbles on the playground and take them with us to the gate. Later on, the assignment became three rocks instead of two. It was Mr. King's diabolically clever scheme to clear the playground of stones. In time, the pile of stones beside the gate grew as big as a small car. I wonder what they finally did with it.

Somewhere I got the idea that Mr. King had some authority during the first war, a drill sergeant perhaps. At times he surely sounded like one. Perhaps on Armistice Day he was remembering some of his old buddies. Vic King really did try hard to teach young boys to be manly and do the "right thing." He was a good man.

Grandpa, who was my mother's father, lived with us and was somewhat entertaining when the subject of the war came up because he always said "bums" when referring to bombs. My brother and I always cracked up (to us, "bums" meant tramps, like Emmett Kelly in the circus). He did do a very useful thing for me once, though: he carefully traced for me three circles, showing the actual diameters of a .30 cal. bullet, a .50 cal., and a 75 mm. cannon shell. For a while that piece of paper, which I still have, made me a big man in my small circle of potential cannon fodder friends.

For we were cannon fodder and we knew it. But (and I know this may be hard for ex-hippies and flower children to accept) we were not in the least bothered by it. We wished we were older. We expected, indeed *longed* for the chance, to get into uniform and join the fight. In 1942 pretty much the whole country felt that way. Or at least said they did.

Everything we kids were exposed to—comic books, radio shows, magazines, newspapers, billboards, movies, and posters at school—promoted going into the military, "doing your duty," or at least helping the war effort somehow. Those who did not were considered shirkers—or worse, cowards. To be rated "4F," which usually meant that you had some physical condition that made you "unfit for military service," was considered somehow shameful and was often referred to (by kids) with a sneer. We couldn't wait to be old enough to get into uniform. We really wanted to get out there and "Gun the Hun" and "Slap a Jap." We really did.

People competed with each other to show how patriotic they were. Sometimes the women were even more energetic than the men.

As far as we were concerned, the rank structure started at Cub Scout, up through Boy Scouts, even Eagle Scout if you could get there—but that was impossible, except for curve-breakers like Buzz Aldrin. (He was about four years ahead of us in school. His older sister once formed what I suppose could be called a brief, intimate acquaintance with my friend Tommy Morgan, when she, driving her car, collided with him on his bike. He says it was his fault and that he has no lasting ill . . . ah . . . ah . . . ah . . . effects.) Then after Scouts, there was second lieutenant in some branch of the military and then on up to—well, what did you want to be?

I always wanted to be a captain myself. There were a lot of captains on the radio. Captain America, Captain Midnight, Captain Silver, Captain . . . you name it. Lots of them.

People do what the Cap'n says to do.

Sometimes.

My only real ambition in life was to be a fighter pilot. Whose wasn't? That came to me around 1940 (during the time of the Battle of Britain). Later on, Captain Midnight and Hop Harrigan and a host of others helped. Hop Harrigan always signed off with a very excited announcer crying, "And remember kids, AMERICA NEEDS FLYERS!"

Chapter 11

Home Front Battles

My parents were definite Anglophiles. My brother and I grew up in a heady atmosphere of talk about how unspeakably horrible the Nazis were, how awful it would be to live under the—in Churchill's fine words—"odious apparatus of Nazi rule," and how brave and noble the British were, fighting this evil with their backs against the wall. The king and queen and two princesses were, well, they were just *marvelous* and showed huge amounts of patrician grit—as the Belgian king was said to have done during World War I, thus perhaps reminding my parents again of their youthful heroes and the fight against the Kaiser.

Which hadn't been so long ago, you know. From 1918 to 1939 is twenty-one years, that's not a very long time. Hell, it's longer than that now back to the first scuffle we had with Saddam Hussein in the desert. So you can see how they must have felt.

"What, *again*? Already?" they must have thought, "Here they come again? How can it happen again so *soon*?" And the obvious next thought would be, "This time we gotta do it *right*! This time we gotta fix them so they *can't* ever do it again!"

Churchill at times spoke of a solution called "Pastoralization." No, that's not something you do to milk. It was a scheme to make all of Germany agricultural and park-like and to forbid any machinery that could be used in any warlike way whatsoever. Roosevelt toyed with an idea called "The Morganthau Plan" for a while, which would have kept Germany completely without industry after the war. Even Ernest Hemingway got into the act, advocating in his book *Men At War* the sterilization of all German males. He said it didn't hurt much at all.

Yes, that's called (gasp) genocide!

Hey, it was 1942. Things were different then. Get a grip.

So there was never any doubt that I, and all of my friends, would go into the military in some way. Matter of fact, we all expected it. All my friends then and in high school, and even for years after that (due to the Korean War), always expected to go into military service somehow. Some didn't much *want* to, but they knew they'd be going.

Some of us did want to go, though. We didn't much relish the idea of all the military chicken-spit, but you have to put up with a lot of crap if you want to fly really hot airplanes.

Even go where nasty people will try to shoot bullets at you? Yup, that too. Nowhere else and no other way could you get to fly such hot airplanes. Nowhere.

But of course, statistically speaking, if there is no war on and they don't need a lot of fighter pilots, no matter how good you are, your chances of actually becoming one are very small. You can pass all the tests, conquer every obstacle, and get through all the weeding out that goes on all the way to getting your wings and your first assignment, and then find out you are not going to get to fly fighters; you've been assigned to fly cargo planes instead.

It happens a lot. But fortunately you don't know that when you're a Cub Scout.

Matter of fact, we may be seeing the last generation of true fighter pilots right now. When your soft little body, with a G-suit's help, can only take about 8G's and the robot machine that is trying to kill you can take 20 or 30, well . . . and then there are laser death rays. They seem to be coming along quite well. Probably it won't be long until we're all carrying Buck Rogers "Zap guns" too. And we won't have to wait until the twenty-fifth century, either. Hot doggies!

It was probably about this time that the ammunition for our weapons dried up. This was a real problem. We would get cap guns as presents for Christmas and birthdays, but caps to load them with became impossible to find. You couldn't get them, nowhere, no how.

After having had caps to fire, it was just not at all satisfying to have to point your weapon at someone and just yell, "Bang! Bang! You're dead!"

Eventually we learned some tricks with kitchen matches. These were "strike anywhere" matches. They were big wooden matches with heads of two colors; the lighter-colored blue part was at the tip and was the part that did the igniting. There was also another kind that were red with white tips. I saw people light them by drawing the tip quickly across the thigh of their jeans like some cowboys did. John Wayne did it, but it was not all that easy to do. I would try it and the match would break, sometimes giving me half a lit match, burning on the floor.

That's not so good if you happen to be standing over the living room rug at the time.

I did learn that you have to hold the match up close to the head to keep it from breaking if you do that, but then you are apt to burn your fingers, which I did, so I didn't try it very often.

But the big thing about those matches was that you could cut the tips off (carefully) and then you had some small explosives that you could hit with a hammer and get a very satisfactory "Whap!"—even louder than a cap gun cap.

By now you may be able to sense where we're going with this. Sure! Make a roll of kitchen match-tips on scotch tape and load them into a cap gun! Obvious! It was pretty hard to get them all stuck on the tape with the correct spacing, and then you'd find out that you needed another layer of tape on top to keep everything from sticking together, but after a lot of frustrating effort, I got it to work. Once. Sort of.

As I remember, the roll wouldn't feed correctly and gave me a lot of trouble. As I write this, I'm wondering why I didn't think to just cut a paper strip and use glue to stick on the match heads. Probably it was a glue problem. We had no airplane glue and everything else took too long to dry. I never thought of nail polish (but that might have led to some uncomfortable questioning from Mom).

Well, it did work, after a fashion. But kitchen match-heads are more powerful than regular caps, and of course I tried to see how loud a bang I could make by putting several in at once.

Yeah, it was louder, all right. It was so powerful that it blew the hammer right off my cap gun and then it would shoot nothing at all. It wouldn't even go click, click. I had another cap gun I was very fond of, a six-shooter revolver modeled after the famous Peacemaker Colt. It took caps in the form of a disk with six caps on it. They were even harder to find than roll caps. I broke the hammer on that one, too.

What good is it to have weapons if you don't have any ammunition? I ask you!

Another use for kitchen matches was a device that I have never seen or heard about anywhere else. This unusual and somewhat exotic form of explosive mayhem was assembled from big nuts and bolts, loaded with some match heads and then thrown high into the sky to hopefully come down on something hard enough to set the match heads off, giving an amazingly loud detonation. Usually the device would come apart and pieces of it would go flying, some of them never to be seen again.

The only people I ever saw using these things were big kids, maybe in eighth or ninth grade.

Just using them to make loud noises was dangerous enough, but I saw some of them thrown toward or near other kids, even once right *at* someone riding a bike!

Impact-fused anti-personnel grenades, you see. The flying bolt could probably have killed if it had hit someone in the head. So, even though we weren't in a combat zone, there were real opportunities to be wounded.

Of course, I did some of my own experiments, but it turned out that for someone in third grade, really big bolts were hard to come by.

Something else we found we could do with kitchen matches was to fire them out of a BB gun into a wall or other hard surface. Incendiary bullets! Yes, they would burst into flame, and, yes, they were fired indoors, but the burning match just fell to the linoleum kitchen floor and was stepped on to put it out. No problem.

But it was probably just as well that no adult ever saw that.

We also found out that you could crunch up a "pop pop cracker" (saltine) in your mouth without getting it wet and then, with your arms out like wings, run around blowing crumbs out of your pursed lips at each other, like tracer bullets. We didn't do this often, I think the hosts had possibly been quizzed by their mother concerning why there were so many crumbs on the kitchen floor.

And if there are any kids reading this, I guess I should tell you, don't try any of these things.

Mom won't like it.

And I beg their mothers' forgiveness.

Most of these experiments took place at the Wells' house. The Wells lived just down the street from us in a big, old Victorian-style house that had just about everything in and on it that four young house apes could use for entertainment. Gary ("Little Wells") was my brother's age, I was about three years older, and Rod ("Big Wells") was about three years older than me. As far back as I can remember Rod was over six feet tall, or at least seemed to be. He wound up at around six foot three. His brother, "Little Wells," eventually topped out even higher and could throw a shot put like it had come out of a mortar.

Their house was a much more interesting place to "play" in than ours was. Ours was just a pretty straightforward, mid-twentieth-century, three-story house with the added inconvenience of usually having my mother around. But after Mrs. Wells got a job in a defense plant, their house was usually free of adult supervision during the day and available for unsupervised mayhem.

The house had a back stairway, with an actual hidden compartment in it. It had other strange passageways, too, and a big, rounded Victorian turret in front with who knew what in it (Charles Addams would have loved it). The big central living room had a fireplace and no ceiling; there was just a balcony that ran all around the circumference, on which you could walk and even drop your younger brother off onto the couch below. That happened at least once, and I don't believe it did the couch much good.

There was also a dark, mysterious basement, which we didn't much want to go down into at all. I was told that there was an actual hidden tunnel down there that went underground under Bradford Avenue to somewhere and had been used during prohibition. Maybe so. I did see the place in the cellar wall—about three feet wide and as tall as a man—where *something* had been walled over.

("For the love of God, Montresor!")

The outside of the house was faced with stones up to the second story, and they were as easy to climb on as the rocks of the cliff. We climbed all over the house, even up to the very peak of the roof, which required some true mountaineering skills.

Another attraction was the garage, which hadn't seen a car for who knows how long, but had a platform beneath the roof just filled to the brim with old newspapers with comic strips in them—a treasure trove!

As 1942 wore on, we began to feel the war entering our lives further and further. Rationing started and soon more and more things were being added to the rationed items list. Mom was issued a ration book full of little stamps, and she had to tear out a few of them to hand in with her money whenever she bought an item of food that was rationed. I think each of us was issued a ration stamp book, but Mom managed them all.

No stamps? No meat!

Sugar was rationed and we had a tray in our house with sugar jars on it, one jar for each person. I think each jar held eight ounces, which was the allotment for each person for a week. You were only allowed to use sugar from your own jar. I think it worked pretty well to teach early lessons about frugality and making things last.

I'm sure butter was rationed, because I well remember the margarine we got. It came in a big mushy, white mass in a plastic bag, with a little spot of red coloring that looked like a drop of blood. What you were supposed to do was break open the little spot of red and knead it into the mass of white margarine until it all mixed up evenly and looked the color of butter. I was asked several times if I wanted to knead the bag of margarine until it was all the right color, but I didn't much like the idea. I had a hard time getting past that drop of blood.

Louise remembers that, too, and she felt like I did about kneading it. She has told me that she once put the bag on a radiator and that it turned all sorts of bizarre unappetizing colors.

Peanut butter had to be mixed, too. When the jar was opened, about an inch or more of oil would be floating on top and you had to get a butter knife or a spatula and dig it into the peanut butter and knead the oil in, trying to mix it up so it would spread easier. If you didn't, the stuff was about the consistency of modeling clay. If your hands weren't big enough to grab the whole jar as you stirred, it could get away from you, and that could be pretty messy.

Mom also bought a new device that was supposed to contribute to victory by doubling our bread supply. As I recall, it had two flat doors, very much like our early toaster, and you put your slice of bread in it, closed the doors that held it vertical, and then, using the special long, thin knife, sliced down through the slice of bread along its flat dimension, thus making one slice into two thinner slices. The special knife sort of interested me, for it had a wavy cutting edge instead of straight. I had never seen a knife like that before. But wavy edge or not, it never worked very well. It was hard to keep the knife right in the middle and get two slices of the same thickness and whatever you did get was apt to be so thin and weak in some areas that it couldn't hold a good helping of peanut butter, say, or jam, and there were some catastrophic structural sandwich failures resulting in an inevitable mess, maybe even on the floor. Recrimination for making these messes was not particularly harsh, maybe because Mom had had the same difficulties herself.

Another thing that was less than satisfactory was that when you tried to toast one of those super thin slices, the area that was thinnest (and there were inevitable thin spots) tended to char, turn into charcoal, and, if not watched closely, even burst into flames sometimes! This, while exciting and entertaining for some of us, did not please management at all, and the war-winning super bread extender eventually disappeared. The super long, thin knife with the wavy edge stayed around for many years, though.

We bought war savings stamps at school, too. We had little books with the spaces all lined off, and we would buy a twenty-five-cent stamp each week and paste it in our books in the right place. After you had amassed a book-full, it was worth $18.75, I think and that would buy a war bond, which would be worth $25.00 when it matured in . . . I don't know, maybe ten years.

I don't think everyone did this; it wasn't compulsory. Some families probably didn't feel like ponying up 25 cents every week for little Johnny or Sally to support the war effort. (Or another one of Roosevelt's nefarious schemes.) But I imagine that those kids who didn't get to do it felt somewhat left out when we were all pasting our stamps in our little books.

Pretty clever, really. I imagine that a quarter a week from even half the school kids in America adds up to a fairly significant piece of change. Probably several million dollars each week.

It cost about $44 million to build an Essex-class aircraft carrier in those days.

Something we did a lot of back then was to trade for various items, at recess usually. Playing cards were popular for a time, but I think it was only cards with neat pictures of clipper ships that were considered valid trading specie—at least that's all I was interested in. I think a lot of moms wondered after a while why they no longer had any full decks of cards in the house when they wanted to play some gin rummy or bridge with their friends. I got urgently questioned once by a schoolmate who was, well, let's say, extremely *agitated* about one playing card she had traded to me. She needed it back right away or, I gathered, her mother was going to . . . make trouble. Well, I had no doubt already traded it away, because Leslie never got her card back. Sorry, Leslie.

The trading craze went on and on, going through permutations with bewildering rapidity. Playing cards, marbles, then fake jewels and jewelry . . . it got to be hard to keep up.

I think it was all a kind of early lesson in capitalism. If you had some of what was desirable at the time, you were popular, and that, I guess, is what is all-important to a kid. It seemed to be a lot of fun at the time. It was a lot like playing monopoly and a little bit like poker.

Another thing you could do with playing cards was to get a spring-loaded clothespin and clip a card or two to one of the braces on the rear wheel of your bike so it would flip against the spokes with a "rat-tat-tat" sound as you rode. This got old pretty quickly. You could get laughed at.

Also there were things called "Big Little Books," which were little books that told a picture story, sort of like comic books, about two inches thick, but only about three by three inches square. I had a lot of fun drawing figures in the upper right side of the pages changing the pose with each page to make them appear to be moving when I rapidly flipped the pages with my thumb. One of my favorites was to make someone jumping out of an airplane and having his parachute open.

Or not.

Something else that appeared were "pocket books." These were regular-length books, but printed on cheaper and thinner paper and cut to a size that would fit in the average pants back pocket or jacket pocket. I think the original intent was to give soldiers something they could easily carry.

Now they are called "paperbacks." The idea seems to have caught on.

I built some models too, but there was no balsa wood anymore; instead there was pine, and it was hard to sand. You'd get a long wing for an airplane and the whole thing had to be sanded down along the trailing edge to make it sharp. You had to do the same thing to the horizontal stabilizer *and* the rudder!

By the time I got to the rudder I'd be really tired of sanding and some pretty sad-looking rudders resulted. There was no longer any decent, fast-drying "airplane glue" to be had either. The glue that came with Strombecker models was awful. It was a yellowish powder in a paper packet. You were supposed to mix it with water, smear it on, clamp it somehow, and leave it overnight. Many times I would pick up my model in the morning only to have it fall apart in my hands. And who wants to wait all that time anyhow? I made a submarine, a Catalina flying boat, and a big B-17, but that was about as far as I cared to go with Strombecker models.

Late in the war, maybe around 1945, balsa wood reappeared and real airplane glue that dried fast became available, too. That stuff was a huge improvement and I made a lot of airplane models after that.

Chapter 12

Sea and Air Battles

In the summer of 1942, things started happening in the Pacific. First there was a big battle between aircraft carriers in the Coral Sea, which was the first in history during which the opposing ships never saw each other. One interesting and unique event during that battle was that when it was nearly dark, several lost Japanese planes tried to land on one of our carriers!

Then, at the beginning of June, there was another battle, north of Midway Island. That was a big one, and a lot of it was kept secret for a while because the main reason we had won was that we had broken the Japanese code. We were not told much, but rumors did start to filter back about it. With good reason, for it had been a tremendously important victory—too good to keep secret for long. It was a real Hollywood sort of story, in which our outnumbered carriers had waited, hidden off to the side, and flight after flight of our obsolete aircraft had attacked and been slaughtered one after the other without even scratching a single enemy ship. Then, at the last moment, two flights of our dive-bombers, unaware of each other, had arrived from different directions, simultaneously and unseen, over the Jap fleet. Diving from high altitude, they attacked and destroyed three enemy carriers almost immediately. Then they went back and got the fourth and last one in the afternoon. Two days later, they sank a large, heavy cruiser and severely damaged another, which was barely able to limp slowly back to Japan. All of this was so miraculous that even Hollywood would probably not have dared to create such a fantastic story line. But it really did happen. It was a tremendous victory, and it changed at one stroke the course of the Pacific War.

Two months later, the battle for Guadalcanal started and lasted for the rest of the year. During the months to come, we were to lose almost as many carriers in the waters around Guadalcanal as the Japs had at Midway, but we also sank some of theirs and damaged others, too. We also sank two of their battleships, but what really hurt them was their loss of pilots. In most of the air battles around Guadalcanal (and there were a lot of them), the Japanese lost more pilots than we did. Most who went down were not recovered. Those pilots had been their "varsity" and they did not have replacements that were as good. They also did not have new carrier construction underway to even remotely approach what we had been building. Our new Essex class carriers started to come out to the Pacific in 1943. They were bigger, faster, and stronger than any that had gone before, and they carried the new Hellcat fighters, which were also bigger, faster, and stronger than any of the Jap airplanes. After 1943 everything in the Pacific changed so much that it seemed almost to be a totally new and different war.

During 1942, the Germans had endured a terrible winter in Russia, unusually cold and severe even for Russia, but when spring came, they had renewed their attack. This time they went more to the south, toward the Caucasus Mountains and the Russian oil fields. Hitler had finally realized that he would need a steady supply of oil to feed his thirsty tanks and airplanes.

One of the things in the way was the Russian city of Stalingrad and the fighting that developed around it became one of the largest battles of the whole war and in the end, a decisive turning point. The battle of Stalingrad went on and on, just like Guadalcanal. It seemed that neither would ever end.

The British were beginning to mount bigger and bigger air raids on Germany, and they had learned how to navigate better. In May, Air Marshal Harris, the new commander of the British bomber force, by using every airplane in his own command and by begging and borrowing from other commands, had scraped together enough machines and crews to mount a 1000-bomber raid on Cologne. The results had been devastating. The city had burned, 45,000 people were now homeless, and there was a certain amount of panic in the population.

But the propaganda effects were greater still. We certainly heard a great deal about it in the newspapers and on the radio. One of the stores in town displayed a large blow-up of a photograph of the twin spires on a famous cathedral in Cologne, fire-blackened and standing alone in a wasteland of burned city. The picture stayed there for several years, I think.

Harris (whose nickname among his bomber crews was "Butch," probably short for "Butcher") tried to make it sound like raids of similar strength would be following regularly, but the truth was that the other commands wanted their airplanes and pilots back and it took quite a while before he could equal such strength on a nightly basis.

That time, however, did eventually come and, as he had foretold, the Germans reaped the whirlwind.

We heard about these things on the radio, of course, but they all seemed very far away. I think our typical second-grade response was something like, "Good, that'll show 'em."

My major concern at the time was, I think, learning to add long columns of figures and finding more pictures of airplanes.

I must have been sick with something, probably chickenpox, and been out of school for a while because there is a permanent hole in my memory concerning nine plus four, and five plus nine, eight, or seven. In those days, it was considered a good thing to get various diseases like measles and chickenpox out of the way when you were young, to get the immunity early. There was also something called a "Schick test," which resulted in a round scab that looked like someone had ground out a cigar in your shoulder. It itched, and we were severely warned not to scratch it. Most of my friends had theirs on their arms, but mine was on my upper thigh. Don't know why.

Down to the east of us, somewhere several miles away towards New York, there was a big hospital or something called "SoHo," which had an ominous sound. It was a sanitorium. People who had things like tuberculosis or polio went there. If you mentioned it, you lowered your voice. It was a place you definitely did not want to be sent to. A regular hospital was bad enough, but SoHo was *serious*.

But over the top of the mountain, in the other direction, only a few miles to the west was an even worse place called "Overbrook." It was a sanitarium. It was for crazy people. Well, it wasn't really filled with crazy, insane, criminal lunatics, but it did hold a certain number of patients who were a little "*adios*," as we used to say out west. But it wasn't what you would call a "maximum security" establishment, and every now and then one of their guests would decide to go AWOL. When that happened, and it was discovered that someone had really and truly gone over the fence, they would set off the most horrible, wailing, up-and-down, gibbering alarm I have ever heard. It wasn't what you'd call a siren really; it was more like an insane shrieking, sobbing, hooting howl that carried and echoed for miles. It easily carried across miles of the valley between the first and second Watchungs, and if you were up in the woods and it was late afternoon when it went off, it could startle you badly. There was a time when Charlie Martin and I were up in the woods and the alarm sounded. "It's the insane asylum!" I yelled, and we both took off like rabbits for the cliff-rim. I had always thought I could move pretty quickly through those woods, but I remember being surprised by how hard it was to keep up with Charlie.

There was another time several years later when some other friends and I, far down in the woods, encountered a somewhat strange young man who was dressed in what looked like a nightgown. He was a little older than we were, quiet, kind of puffy and soft looking, had a sort of embarrassed smile, and didn't seem threatening at all. We talked with him a little and it turned out that what he wanted most in life was to be burned with matches. It did strike us as pretty odd, but we hadn't heard any alarm sirens and he seemed to be nice and gentle . . . so we obliged him. Once. With a match than had gone out. I didn't do the actual application, but I do very well remember the hiss of the match on the skin of his chest. He writhed a bit in what looked to me like fake pain. He thanked us and so we left him. I don't think we ever did hear any sirens go off for that one. He seemed to be lost.

My mother also met a few. Our house was sort of at the end of the line. After us there was the quarry and then the woods that extended from the top of the quarry down into the valley to the west where Overbrook was. When a runaway got tired of wandering around barefoot in the woods, they would come and knock on the door and ask Mom if they could use the telephone. She always let them use it or would use it herself and would then offer them some lemonade and sit there chatting with them until the people with the nets arrived.

Well . . . they didn't *really* come with nets. I just threw that in, but you know what I mean. The unexpected guests certainly didn't frighten her. Mom was not what you'd call timid.

She once heard one say on the phone, "Well, Dad, I did it again." Which would seem to indicate that he either wasn't watched very closely, or was an extremely clever escape artist.

Another thing that seemed strange to us was that one day, an olive-drab telephone in a box appeared on a tree in the woods. It was fairly close to the edge of the cliff, and the wire to it led over the side of and away from the cliff and down toward the houses below. Then a while later, we met some men up there with binoculars who just stood around, looked out toward New York, and seemed bored. I bet they did get bored, for there was usually not much going on but the occasional DC-3 going into Newark. In the winter, in the late afternoon up there on the cliff-rim with a wind blowing, it could get plenty cold.

It was not long before the young men on lookout disappeared, but the telephone stayed there throughout the war. Many of us were tempted to pick it up and see who answered, but I don't know anyone who had the courage to do that. This wasn't just run-of-the-mill "I dare ya" stuff, you know, this was *military*.

CHAPTER 13

Adventures with Mom

Mom would pile me into the car from time to time and we would go on expeditions together. I don't know what she did about my brother, and I don't know how she got the ration stamps or the gas to go on these trips, and I'm not quite sure what the reason for them was. Maybe she just got a touch of cabin fever from time to time. Possibly the stamps were some leftovers at the end of the month.

One time we went out to Morristown to see Washington's headquarters, and another time we went to a place with a funny name: Jenny Jump State Forest. We even went to a place called Stokes State Forest, which seemed to be a long way away on the western border of the state. I remember getting tired on that one, and I have no idea why we went there. Maybe Mom was just bored.

She also took me into New York quite often, and most of the time I didn't want to go because it meant I had to get "dressed up." I realize now that she was "exposing" me to things, things that had to do with "culture." We went to various art museums, including the Metropolitan Museum of Art. I particularly remember a painting by Andrew Wyeth in which the viewpoint of the observer was up in the air, looking down on a soaring bird—a vulture I think—and down below the vulture was a field. I had never seen a painting done from that point of view and was greatly impressed. I thought it was wonderful. It gave the viewer a real feeling of being airborne, of flying. I think this was at the Museum of Modern Art and the memory actually even be from right after the war ended. I still think it's a fine painting. Another Wyeth that impressed me and which I think I first saw then was "Wind From the Sea" which is simply an open window in a house near the sea, with the light, airy curtains blowing in toward the viewer. It can almost make you feel the relief of a cooling breeze on a hot summer day.

On these trips, we would often take the subway to get where we were going, and I always liked to stand at the front of the first car looking out the window at the tracks and lights sailing toward us. It could be nearly hypnotic.

I think we used the subway so much because we would park the car at, or take a bus to, Hoboken and then ride the ferryboat across the river. I really enjoyed riding the ferry, not only because of all the interesting things you could see on the river (sometimes even really *big* ships), but also because the landing, when we came in to the ferry slip, was always a sort of half-controlled crash that made the big pilings groan and sway and look like they were going to break.

Mom always made me wash my hands thoroughly, maybe even take a bath, after we got home, to wash off the city grime. And judging from the color the water turned, that was a good idea! She always called New York "The Great and Wicked City," but you could see that she relished it.

We also took a trip down to Red Bank one day to see Betty Merriam, a friend of Mom's who I think was a fellow flower-arranger. Since pleasure trips were frowned upon by the "authorities" who rationed gasoline, I imagine Mom must have justified this trip as being some kind of war work because we were going to help harvest vegetables. I was promised I'd get to see Fort Monmouth, which was nearby and "might have some tanks and airplanes at it." The Merriams seemed to have a very large yard; perhaps it was even a farm. It certainly had a lot of things growing on it, and we, along with the Merriams' son, picked many string beans that day. The main thing I remember about them was that they seemed to be very *large* string beans.

We did make a tour of Fort Monmouth, but not one tank did I see. I sure saw a lot of soldiers, though. The beach was nearby, but we were told there was no hope of getting out on it. We couldn't even go to see it. I think civilians were not allowed. Later that day, I heard some pretty wild stories from the Merriams' son and one of his friends about the wartime wreckage that washed up on the beaches.

Mrs. Merriam came to visit Mom at our house, too, at least once that I recall. She was quite dressed up, maybe going to some meeting, and she was wearing a small white hat with a little net in front of her eyes. I wondered some about that. What was it for? It certainly wouldn't keep bugs from getting in her eyes, or birds, either. I was much impressed by her eyes. They appeared to be a very pale blue, almost violet.

She seemed to be a very nice lady.

Mom would often, but not always, pick us up from school at noon and take us home for lunch, especially in winter. Sometimes I'd get distracted and would be a little late finishing my meal. I'd look at the clock and realize I had to be back to class in ten minutes, so I'd take off running. It was mostly downhill, almost a mile, and I'd run the whole way, which I think may have helped me later, playing soccer. Often I would gulp down my glass of milk just before I took off, and from my mother's horrified exclamation, I got the impression that she thought this was life-threatening. But there were never any ill effects. My stomach did make some sloshing noises as I ran, though.

Once when Mom brought me home there was a big mystery in the kitchen. She had left two eggs boiling on the stove when she went out, but they had disappeared! The dry saucepan was still there, and the low flame was still burning under it, but the water was gone and there was no trace of the eggs. None. She looked all over the kitchen for them, and so did I. Then I looked at the ceiling. There were two eggs plastered neatly to the ceiling above the stove. They must have simply gotten so hot that they just exploded upward. They looked just like two fried eggs on a plate would look, the flat white surrounding the yolk, all very neat, no mess, no splatter. But stuck to the ceiling. Mysteriously, there was no trace that I could see of the shells. Very strange. A fun memory.

There was another time when she picked me up and I could tell that something was different. She seemed excited and her eyes were shining. When we got home, she showed me what she had: a blue ribbon with some writing on it in white ink. She had won first place for a flower arrangement at a flower show. It was her first one! She was quite proud of it, but I'm afraid I didn't act impressed enough. I wasn't very interested in flowers; I was into airplanes. I wish now that I had acted more excited, but at any rate, I was the first person she showed it to.

In years to come that scene would be repeated many, many times. In fact, she won so often that they kicked her upstairs, made her a judge so she couldn't compete any more. So she took to writing books and giving lectures about flower arranging instead.

Many years later, after she was gone and I was cleaning out the house, I opened the bottom drawer of her desk and was astonished. The whole drawer, four feet wide and at least two feet deep, was crammed solid, completely *full* up to the top with ribbons she had won, and a great many of them were blue.

The honest truth is that it didn't dawn on me until I was about forty years old that my mother was a little bit unusual—that she did things most other moms didn't do. That thought hit me when I heard someone talking about how deeply he hated his own mother. I was truly shocked! A strong feeling of *wrong* came over me. I imagine what I felt it must be like for a deeply religious person to hear something they consider blasphemy. At that moment, I suddenly realized how wonderful my mother really was and all that she had done for me.

But when I was younger, I never gave it much thought. My father could draw anything and paint very good watercolors, and Mom could play the piano and knew everything there was to know about flowers and how to put them in a vase and win flower shows. That was all.

She did often say, "I have no artistic talent at all, I can't even draw a straight line."

And then my brother and father and I would all hoot and laugh and carry on, trying with our overdone false derision to let her know just how very artistic we knew she really was.

I don't remember how old you had to be to become a Cub Scout, maybe nine, but the age came and my friends and I all joined up. At the time it was just the thing to do. I think we may have seen it as a first step toward the military. You did get to wear a uniform and get decorations—that was a big incentive.

I suppose Mom thought that it might be fun, or a "good" thing to do, to be a den mother, so she became the den mother for myself and a number of my friends who made up our "pack." Part of it, I think, was that she genuinely liked her pack of young cubs (and they certainly liked her). She probably thought that the quarry and the woods above it would be a good place for us to learn woodcraft skills. Under her direction, we no doubt engaged in a number of fine projects, but about all I remember now are a few excursions we made up into the woods.

On one such occasion, I was supposed to be the "hare" and the rest of the pack were the "hounds." They were supposed to track me, and I was to leave a trail of pieces of paper. I well remember that time, because it was a hot summer day and I had a toothache. The more I ran, the more the tooth throbbed, and that led to a headache. I began to feel awful, but these were *my* woods; I couldn't possibly let them catch me. It would be shameful. So I ran and tore my pieces of paper, which cost time, and my toothache got worse and worse. They never did catch me, but it was a pounding, painful run in the hot sun that I'll never forget.

One of our cub pack was Walt Davis. Walt was always a foot taller than anyone else. He still is. One day, after we had finished with whatever project we had been doing, the rest of us were about a hundred feet away from Walt when he picked up the biggest branch he could find and came roaring up the slope at us like a berserk monster. Funny thing is, we all knew perfectly well that it was just Walt, but for a second it really did panic us and we ran like rabbits.

Chapter 14

Pet Words and Wildlife

One of the things that we did in those days to further the war effort was to collect the big, steel, quart-sized cans that tomato juice and grapefruit juice came in, cut the tops and bottoms off and stomp the cans flat on the floor. I always liked to do the stomping. Mom would take the cans somewhere to be turned into airplanes and tanks. She also saved bacon fat and other grease from cooking, which was also turned in eventually to make something out of—I don't remember what it was (maybe Glycerin), but I had the idea it was some kind of explosive.

She also saved bacon fat to fry french fries in. She didn't cut french fries the way you see them now, strips that would be square in cross section. She cut the potato in half and then sliced across the half-potato so that all the pieces were crescent shaped. I am aware that doing french fries in bacon fat is not now correct-think, but believe me, those fries done in bacon fat tasted better than what we get now—*much* better—and I think the crescent shape made them better, too. You should try it sometime.

Mom had some pet words and sayings that I have never heard anywhere else, so I guess she must have made them up. When someone had an upset stomach, for instance, she said they (or she) were feeling "icky in the garden," which, for me at least, could conjure up all sorts of strange scenarios. She also had a term for the material you might find on your upper lip when you had a cold and had sneezed violently. She called it "Mugoozalum."

Unfortunately, she often used that word to describe the white of an egg when it was not fully cooked. I have not been able to stand underdone eggs since.

I think some of the other terms she used came from an earlier era. She would say that something was "on the fritz" if it wasn't working and would call me "snigglefritz" at times. She would also call me—or anyone else who had done something stupid—a "dumb cluck."

My theory is that some of these terms might have harkened back to the First World War, which had started when she was ten. The Germans were then often called "Fritzes." There was also a German General named Von Kluck, who, during their invasion of France, commanded the far right wing of the German Army. In fear of being outflanked, he had turned his army to the east before he got to Paris, thus ruining their whole invasion plan. Maybe a lot of people talked about that for a while, hence "dumb cluck."

Maybe so, maybe not so. How do *I* know? I'm only six. On the other hand, maybe it had something to do with chickens. As I said, it's just a theory.

My father would say things like "Now you're cookin' with gas," and "Aw, that's the bunk!" I suppose the first one must have come from the days when gas lines were put in and people could stop cooking over wood stoves or with coal, but that would make it from at least the generation before his. Maybe he got it from his father. Where the "bunk" came from is a mystery to me. I have seen terms such as "bunkum" and "Bunko-Steerers" used in ways that seemed to describe something false, but that's about as far as I can go.

He would tell me to "shut yer yap" from time to time (I was probably a pretty mouthy little kid), but the one that really baffled me was when he would tell me to "go pee up a rope."

Never could figure that one out. Seems to me you'd get wet.

Although there were various other houses around us, there were also many large trees and the real woods started just west of us and ran all along the ridgeline to the north and south. There was plenty of wildlife in the woods, even though we were only about fifteen miles west of the city. I had often seen deer up there. There were raccoons and woodchucks, too, and one cold morning while in the kitchen, my father in great excitement started yelling at us to come look because two bald eagles had landed up on top of the south cliff. I saw their white heads myself—they really were eagles—but I never saw any there again.

Another thing we had were screech owls, which make a sort of high, shivering, descending call. They don't say anything that sounds like a "hoot" at all. I often heard them after I had gone to bed. One was calling in the woods one night when my father came into my room and emphatically told me that the sound was *not* a ghost, but was a screech owl. Well, that was interesting. The thought that it might be a ghost had never entered my mind. I knew what it was.

Like my mother, I have always thought of owls as good luck and especially enjoy hearing a pair of them on a crisp fall evening, hooting back and forth to each other in the moonlit woods.

Another kind of wildlife that we had a lot of (in the summer) were mosquitoes.

I sometimes wonder now if the people enjoying football games in the Meadowlands Stadium have any idea that they are sitting where there once really were meadows (though I always did think that they should have been called swamplands instead of meadowlands). You could see them from on top of the cliff if you knew where to look—a thin, yellow line on the hazy blue-gray land, way out there toward the city. When we went into the city we would cross the meadows, several miles it seemed of waving tall grass and reeds. What was below the ten-foot-high grasses was water. Water and mosquitoes.

Before they were drained, the Jersey Meadows were the home and breeding grounds for billions of mosquitoes. Those mosquitoes were a big and hardy breed capable of flying anywhere they needed to go to find some naked human flesh to feed on.

At home in the summertime, we'd almost always have one or two of them in the room with us after we'd gone to bed. All my friends say the same thing about their homes. I don't know how they got in. All the windows and doors were open during the day to let the air in, but they all had screens on them. Of course, there were probably gaps, and, of course, what else does a hungry mosquito have to do all day but probe and probe and try to get inside where it can smell live *people*?

Remembering the many nights I lay on my bed, sweltering in the heat and miserable humidity, unable to get to sleep (nobody had air conditioning then), I have wondered why in the world I didn't just open the door and open the window across the hall from my door to at least get a cross-draft? The answer, I guess, is that I didn't want to let any more mosquitoes in. And they would find you; they followed your breath to your face. Once you had lain in wait (using yourself as bait), and finally nailed the one or two that were tormenting you, you didn't want to risk it, because for me anyhow, it was just about impossible to get to sleep if I had one of them whining here and there in my room, sometimes closer, sometimes farther away.

I would lie on my back, tense, ready to strike, then I'd feel the tiny brush on my face and *BLAP!* The killing blow . . . or maybe not. Possibly great remorse instead, because I had either just hit myself, *hard*, on the face for nothing, or maybe worse, had succeeded and now had mushed mosquito somewhere on my face, which was hard to stop thinking about.

CHAPTER 15

Radio: The Window to Everywhere

Radio was our entertainment during the war years; there was no television yet.

There was a man though, named DuMont, who lived nearby. He was an early television pioneer and had built what looked like a sort of castle up on top of the ridgeline a little south of us. From there he had direct line-of-sight to the Empire State Building and conducted many early experiments with TV. I think that possibly some of the searchlights I had seen had been located somewhere up near there, maybe even on his front lawn!

There were all sorts of radio shows, but the ones we kids were mainly interested in were what you'd call "adventure" shows. I think we've lost a lot with stories now being prepackaged for us by television. Now we see on the screen what some model-maker's idea of a hideous monster or an alien spaceship is. But when you only have your own imagination to work with and Buck or the Captain (with perhaps Betty or Joyce) comes up against some horrible, hideous, slimy monster, your mind automatically conjures up whatever you yourself consider most horrible and hideous, and I think the illusion is more effective that way.

The illusions were aided greatly by the sound-effects men. I eventually formed a medium fascination with how the noises were made, and I studied up on the subject. I learned about crackling cellophane for fire, dropping rice quickly or slowly on a hard surface for rain, rippling a big piece of sheet metal for thunder (turns out you need a really *big* piece of sheet metal to do that). And I sent away for and still have a stack of thin steel plates which, when dropped on a hard floor behind someone, sound exactly like breaking glass or platters. I was able to startle several family members with that one, but was usually *firmly* asked not to do it again. Or else.

Well here we are. It's almost five o'clock, we're sitting by the radio with our comic book and maybe a small airplane model and our decoder badge, and we're ready!

Suddenly, *BONG!* A big bell starts tolling. *BONG. BONG. BONG.* (I think they probably used a recording of Big Ben in London. We heard that at other times on the radio, too, maybe New Year's.) And off in the distance you could hear it coming, an airplane (*rrrrrrooooow*) getting closer, getting closer. *BONG. BONG.* He's going into a dive now (aaarrrrrrrrr RRRRROOOAAAAW), and the announcer, very excited, is howling, "CAP—"*BONG!*"—TAYN—" *BONG! RRRAAAAOOOW!* (the airplane is very loud now, pulling out right over our heads) "—MID-NIIIIIYTE!" *BONG, BONG, BONG, BOOOOONNNG! Rooooowrrroooowwummmmm!* (The bell fades; the airplane fades into distance.)

Ow-Moi-Gaw-ed! It was so exciting! A little kid would just about . . .

Well, no, he wouldn't really, because after a few times it was just good ole Cap'n Midnight flying into the living room again. Flying in with Billy or Bucky (or was he one of Jack Armstrong's young friends?) and Joyce (I have always liked the name Joyce ever since) and Ikky (Ichabod Mudd—Captain Midnight's rough-hewn but theoretically lovable mechanic—one of the most ridiculous characters a kid who was planning to fly P-38s and tangle with the Luftwaffe ever had to mentally deal with. He spoke with a badly done Brooklyn accent. In those days all mechanics did. Brooklynites were everywhere: in the movies, comic books, and adventure stories too.) who all helped Captain Midnight struggle with his arch enemy Ivan Shark, or Nazis, or Japs for ten minutes or so, because you had to endure a commercial or two for Ovaltine as well ("Who but the Swiss . . . ").

Why the Swiss? What made this sort of odd-tasting fake chocolate milk the Swiss had come up with so wonderful? It tasted like it was part dried carrots. Was that because they were surrounded and cut off by evil enemies in Europe? I didn't really much like the taste of the stuff. (Once, when visiting my cousin Ted, however, I watched him stealthily climb up on the counter, reach up into the cupboard, get down a can of Ovaltine powder, and, making sure his mother couldn't hear him, eat a few spoonfuls of it right out of the can! I got the impression that he actually *liked* the stuff and was forbidden from doing that very often. Yow!)

But I had to drink a lot of it. Mom said I had to drink it if she bought it, and you had to do *that* if you wanted a *label*, and you had to have a *label* to send in with your *dime* to get to the point of the whole exercise, which was the incredibly valuable prize (here it is, the really exciting part): the *bygawd* SECRET DECODER BADGE! Some years the badge would have a tiny mirror embedded in the middle, to signal to your buddies in airplanes overhead—from your life raft I guess—or to see what plots were being hatched behind your back in school (yes, that's you, Tommy). Other years it would have a magnifying glass, perhaps, maybe to roast ants with, or other things, but the whole *bygawd* point was to be able to decode the *secret messages*!

So there you were, the program was ending and, suddenly horrified, nearly too late, you'd realize you had to have a piece of paper and a pencil ("MOM!"). Then you'd tensely hunch over the radio, carefully transcribing the *secret* message that only the *faithful* members of the "Secret Squadron" could decode. The announcer's voice would drone: "D . . . Sixteen . . . R . . . Twenty-two . . . K . . . Eight . . . " and so on. You would laboriously decipher it with your secret decoder badge and you would see the amazing, magic, secret message slowly appear on your pad and it would say, perhaps (in an incredible piece of marketing department chicanery), "Drink Ovaltine."

I believe that was the first (but hardly the last) time I've felt what you might call the "sting of American sales promotion."

Kinda foolish, really. Even a little kid will wise up after being conned a few times, and then he (or she, for there were girls in the secret squadron, too) wouldn't save up pennies and get Mom to buy that stuff anymore! But I suppose the real point of it all was to be able to send secret messages to various friends who were also in the secret squadron. Important messages like "Miss Goombah has bad breath," or "What's answer 9?"

I don't recall ever using the badge to do that; it was just a cool thing to have. Actually using it to encode messages was kind of a drag.

If you did have a dime and didn't send it in to Captain Midnight or somebody else, that ten cents could buy a lot of root-beer flavored Paloops (a flat lollypop with a sort of oval, soft paper-fiber loop for a handle instead of a stick) or Necco Wafers or Bazooka Bubble Gum or even, yes, Walnettos.

Walnettos weren't so bad, either: caramel with little chunks of walnut (I guess) in them. A whole row of little squares, each in its own wax paper wrapper. Maybe ten of them. For a nickel. Pretty good deal for a nickel! (Or was it a dime?) You can still find them if you know what high-priced catalog to look in, but they sure aren't ten for a nickel anymore.

The term "cost-effective" hadn't been invented by Bobby MacNamara yet, but we learned young; we understood it. We'd spend long minutes looking at the candy rack in the corner store, driving Mrs. Lempert insane, trying to decide.

There were lots of little trinkets offered to the kiddies by the radio shows of those days. All involved sending in a dime usually, but also the all-important box top or label. That, of course, was the real point, to get Mom to buy a box or a jar of whatever it was so you could get the label. Then Mom would say you had to drink or eat the stuff. Wheaties weren't so bad (that's what Jack Armstrong was pushing), and the Lone Ranger wanted you to eat Cheerios, but sometimes I could get pretty tired of Ovaltine.

I think it was Jack Armstrong who once offered a "glow-in-the-dark Dragon Ring," which was probably my all-time favorite. It was just a little white plastic ring with what was supposed to be a dragon's eye in the middle and if you held it close to a light for a few seconds it would soak up enough light to then glow in the dark for a while with an eerie green glow. It probably went for a dime and a Wheaties box top. The last time I checked, about thirty years ago, if you had one that was still in its cellophane wrapper it was worth about $400.00!

An odd thing happened when I got that ring out and looked at it in the dark again after many years had passed. A weird feeling swept over me, and I was at a loss to identify what it was (and that in itself can make you feel pretty strange, having a strong feeling and not knowing what it is). I guess for a few seconds I had popped right back to 1943, and the eerie green glow of the little plastic ring was wonderful and magic once again.

The feeling quickly passed, though, and has never returned, of course, I have tried to recapture it. I suppose it only happens when you open a door to memory that has been closed for a long time.

Smells will do that. The smell of smoke from burning leaves, and, as I've said, the smell of kerosene can sometimes take me back. Mom used Hines' honey and almond lotion and lily-of-the-valley perfume, and they'll do it too.

I wonder if that ring will still glow in the dark a thousand years from now? I bet it will.

Another thing that was offered by somebody—seems to me it was Wheaties again, but Ovaltine or Captain Midnight would make more sense—were paper airplanes printed on heavy paper with authentic colors and markings. They had a wingspan of about a foot, and you'd cut them out and glue them together, with a penny in the nose for weight, then tie a string to the wing tip and whirl them around your head to make them fly. They really would fly, too, if you didn't overdo it. I think I had a P-40 and a Jap Zero. I'm afraid they didn't last very long, though. They were both destroyed by "uncontrolled flight into terrain" (pilot error).

Sometimes I thought the hucksters went a little too far, like when Captain Midnight offered a device that was touted to act like a telescope when you looked through it at distant objects. What it amounted to was an empty paper tube. True, it would isolate the object you were looking at and perhaps make you think you could see more detail, but it was really just a tube. The cardboard tube from inside a roll of paper towels, even from a roll of toilet paper, would do just as well. I didn't bother getting that one.

Right after the war ended, everyone was naturally very excited about atomic energy. Some genius came up with the idea for an "atomic ring," which had a tiny little magnifying lens in it and some radioactive material and some phosphorescent stuff that would make flashes when energetic particles hit it. You could see them best in the dark. I had one and it did make flashes. I wonder, did those rings contribute at all to some of the cataracts kids of my generation have gotten?

There were lots of radio shows. *Lots.* About the earliest one I remember was some kind of "club" for really little kids, run by someone who called himself "Uncle Don." ("Ho-de-ko DOAKS with an-alla-ka-ZON, sing this song with your Uncle Don" for those who may have forgotten.) Nancy and I listened to this together a few times. But one day Uncle Don accidentally said a *baaad* thing, not realizing that he still had a live microphone, and pretty soon after that, Uncle Don went bye-bye.

But by that time there were other shows to listen to that were *much* better.

There were several other networks, and they all ran their fifteen-minute shows during the same hour. It seems to me that the whole magic hour started at six p.m., but that can't be right, it would have interfered with supper. Must have been five.

At least two networks ran four fifteen-minute programs, one right after the other. If you didn't have a favorite, the choice could paralyze you. It might have been *Jack Armstrong, All-American Boy* ("Sing a song of Hudson High, boys, show them how we stand . . . "), or, of course, *Captain Midnight.* Or it could have been *Captain Silver* (there seemed to be a lot of captains around in those days). One I never missed was *The Adventures of Hop Harrigan.* Hop's adventures nearly always involved airplanes and at the end of the show, the last thing the announcer excitedly yelled was, "And remember, kids, AMERICA NEEDS FLYERS!" A message it seems I took to heart.

There was also *Terry and the Pirates,* but I didn't pay Terry much mind. I was interested in airplanes, and as I recall, Terry was always splashing around on the water then. And his part-time nemesis, the Dragon Lady, I believe lived at least some of the time on a boat, an opulent Chinese junk of some kind. A really *big* one with secret passageways. Terry later became heavily involved with flying and spent some time messing around with the Flying Tigers, I think, but by then it was too late: I had outgrown the five-to-six bunch.

There was a cluster of other shows that aired before five o'clock, too. *Stella Dallas, Backstage Wife* and *Lorenzo Jones and His Wife, Belle* are two that I remember. I have no idea what they involved, but it wasn't airplanes. They did sell soap powder, though, thus reinforcing the term "soap opera."

Some of those commercials (which you'd accidentally hear if you turned the radio on early, so as not to miss any important *Captain Midnight* time) could get in your mind and stick. Stick for seventy years or more, as a matter of fact. There was the ditty "Rinso white! Rinso bright! Happy little washday song!" with a cutesy little whistle thrown in. (Even at that age I thought the idea of happy housewives prancing around in the laundry room was absurd.) And there was Lifebuoy Soap, endlessly funny because of the foghorn voice that said "Beee-OOOOooooh" in a deep voice that sounded like a long, *long* burp.

One commercial that has always stuck with me was for Doan's Pills (not to be confused with Carter's Little Liver Pills), which would protect you from those awful-sounding things: the deadly duo of "neuritis" and "neuralgia." I didn't know what they were—I still don't—but I sure didn't want any! Evidently, if you got either, it was just about all over for you. I remain pretty leery about them both.

I must have gotten so familiar with that commercial because it aired just before one of my favorite shows came on. I also have a clear memory of eating breakfast cereal—puffed rice—while listening to Jack Armstrong. Why would that be? Mom would never have given me breakfast cereal for supper . . . unless I was sick and it (with milk and cut-up bananas on it) was thought to be restful for the stomach. I seem to remember being in pajamas and a bathrobe, too, so that must be it.

Mom used to express amazement that I (and my brother) could eat supper, listen to the radio, read a comic book, and draw pictures all at the same time. But that wasn't so much. I find it a lot harder now to understand what some talking head on TV is babbling about while absorbing the meaning of the words scrolling across the bottom of the screen. But of course, a lot of what happens around a kid is just noise and goes right over them.

There were times, I remember, when some adult would point out that I hadn't moved for a while, and was just sitting perfectly still—perhaps even with a spoonful of something halfway to my mouth—as if I were paralyzed or in some sort of a trance. That, I guess, is apt to get a parent's attention. Not to worry, Mom, it's just that someone—the good Captain, or Hop, or Jack

Armstrong—was doing something really *interesting* at that point, like making nitroglycerin out of soap to blow the lock off a dungeon door, for instance. That could really get your attention! If it worked, it could be useful!

Then there was *The Lone Ranger*. Seems to me he might have been on Saturdays. Someone once said that the definition of a true intellectual is "a person who can hear the introduction to the William Tell Overture and not think of *The Lone Ranger*."

I think that's pretty keen.

I don't know how long he'd been around, but I do know that he had ridden out of the pages of yesteryear by the time of the 1939 World's Fair.

An interesting character, the Lone Ranger. What a concept! A man—at a time and place in history when outlaws were fairly common—who rides constantly from town to town, wearing a *mask*, thus immediately putting everyone who met him (or even saw him from a distance), on edge for fear of being robbed. He also must have been somewhat paranoid about werewolves because he used only silver bullets. He carried a whole gun-belt full of them, evidently. (You would think that this might have made *him* a frequent target for robbers, wouldn't you? Maybe that's how he got to be such a good shot— constant practice.) He rode "a fiery horse with the speed of light . . . " Well, that must have made it pretty hard for Tonto to keep up, huh?

Tonto, his Indian sidekick, said something like "Tiyo, Keemosavvy" a lot and also something like "Unnnguhuh," both of which are somewhat tricky to translate. In comic books, the noise Tonto made was written simply as "Ugh!" which made it look like he was periodically getting punched in the gut by something unseen. Or maybe Tonto had an ulcer. I bet he did; he did lead a pretty stressful life, after all, what with trying to keep up, and his boss being a werewolf-paranoid weirdo, and being punched in the gut by ghosts all the time . . . it couldn't have been an easy life for good ole Tonto.

A lot of radio and comic book characters said "Great Scott!" when amazed by something. I'm not quite sure about the Lone Ranger, but Captain Midnight said it, and many others did, too. I sometimes wondered whom, exactly, they were referring to. Was it Sir Walter Scott? Was it Robert the Bruce? Bruce the Robert? I don't know. You don't hear it much any more. People don't say it. You could get laughed at.

During the war and after, there was a comic book and radio character called the Green Hornet—(not to be confused with the Green Lantern). In "reality" his name was Britt Reed. The Green Hornet fought crime like everybody else and had an amazingly powerful, shiny black limousine called the Black Beauty, driven by his faithful Japanese chauffeur and lackey, Kato.

News of a crime would come in and "Great Scott!" our hero would cry. "Get out the Black Beauty, Kato!"

"Ahso, Missa Blitt!" Kato would alertly answer, leaping chop-chop into action. The garage door, which was disguised as a storefront, would swing open, and with a loud, howling buzz (like an angry hornet, see?) the Black Beauty would sweep off down the boulevard (hopefully missing any astonished citizens who might have been strolling by on the sidewalk when the garage door flipped up).

Kato's ancestry miraculously changed from Japanese to Filipino shortly after December 7, 1941. An amazing metamorphosis, I admit, but even more amazing than that, I think, is the Green Hornet's genealogy. It turns out, you see, that Missa Blitt's great-grand-uncle Reed, back in the late 1800s, had been a man of mystery who rode around fighting crime in the old west. He was known as (brace yourselves) . . . the Lone Ranger!

Pretty amazing, huh?

There is someone who also calls himself the Green Hornet on TV now, but he's not the real one.

The Lone Ranger had what I thought of as an "announcer voice." Low, but filled with sincere urgency, sort of projected from the back of the throat, authoritative, with a touch perhaps of Vaughn Monroe. During the war and for a while after it, radio announcers all sounded like that. And movie narrators too—really serious, authoritative, and a bit arrogant, I thought. Either they all imitated each other, or they were picked because they sounded like that, or maybe they were all actually the same guy! But they all sounded a lot like the Lone Ranger.

Orson Wells could sound that way. Maybe they were all trying to imitate him. He made like he was an announcer when he did that famous *War of the Worlds* show that panicked a lot of people on the East Coast. Some people right around where we lived got pretty clanked up because the Martians had supposedly landed in a town to the south of us, near Princeton. A few people got in their cars and went up to Eagle Rock, which is nearby and has a fine view of the city, to see what was going on, but all they saw was a bunch of other semi-freaked-out people. There were some automobile accidents, and I understand that a farmer down near Grover's Mill saw the town water tower coming for him and took a shot at it. He winged it, too.

I don't actually remember hearing that show. I was undoubtedly in bed, but I do remember a few times when my father seemed somewhat agitated and secretive and would now and then nip outside to take a look around. Maybe this was one of those times. I have a recording of that broadcast.

Orson's voice was really something.

He was also the voice of *The Shadow* for some of the early episodes. Not to take anything away from whomever did the later shows, but Orson's voice was something else entirely! When he said, "The weed of crime bears *bitter* fruit," you sure believed it *did*, baby! And then there was The Shadow's laugh! Ow, moi, Gaw-ed! You have to hear old Orson do *that* to really appreciate what is possible for the human voice. It's on another recording. It's scary.

The Shadow's girlfriend, Margo Lane, worked with him and helped him solve crimes. Sometimes she even got to whack an evildoer over the head with whatever was handy, maybe her shoe. She was not called a "girlfriend," however; she was a "friend and traveling companion" to Lamont Cranston, another one of those playboys or "men about town." When you could see him, that is. When it was time to fight crime, he could go invisible and become The Shadow. It was an old trick he'd picked up in the Orient. That's some trick, all right. Quite helpful in a fight, being invisible.

Since Margo and Superman's girlfriend, Lois Lane, both had the same last name, for a long time I suspected that they were sisters, working the radio show and "traveling companion" bit together. I wonder, do you suppose there were ever any uncomfortable questions from curious relatives at family get-togethers? "Oh Margo, dahling . . . could you help us out just a teensy bit? It's just that it's been so terribly *vague*, dear, and we've all been wondering. Just what exactly does a 'traveling companion' actually *do*, dear?"

Buck Rogers now, he was in the twenty-fifth century and flew around in space in his spaceship called "The El Dorado," and I liked that a lot because The El Dorado had a hull made of SOLID GOLD. You know, but *painted* so nobody could ever find out. That's how Buck hid his wealth from the enemy. I wonder if he ever accidentally scratched some of the paint off in a hard landing?

Thinking about that now, I think maybe Buck was onto something. A hull made of gold might have protected them from a lot of radiation. You know . . . until it started to emit secondaries.

Now Buck, he had an old scientist friend with a bald, egg-shaped head and thick, coke-bottle glasses, whose name was Dr. Huer. Dr. Huer spoke in a very dry, reedy voice and said, "Heh!" a lot. He figured out neat weapons and other scientific stuff for Buck to use.

One time, they were up against some really *serious* bad-news aliens, some nemesis that was a really potent and fearful enemy, one that might even *win* (and then, of course, where would we be?), an enemy that was so awful and hideous that they even scared Buck and his crew, who would say things like

"Arrrgh!" and "Aiee!" when they saw them. They encountered this enemy right there in the laboratory with them! Buck and company were horrified because the aliens were so awful looking, and I got the idea that they were like giant insects. It seems to me that they came out of the machines or electronic equipment somehow. You could also hear the horrible noise they made! At that point, they became believable, even to me at the other end of the radio. It was *scary*! It really was a hideous noise—a kind of horrible screechy metallic howl—and I didn't like it.

And then, sometime, maybe weeks later, I was home, still in my pajamas, probably had a cold, maybe a little feverish. Mom had gotten a call on the upstairs phone, then gone out in a hurry on some errand. So I was lying there on my bed, alone in the house, probably looking at my airplane scrapbook, when an awful, hideous noise started out low and built up slowly from somewhere frighteningly close. It was a long, drawn-out, metallic, wailing screech. It swelled up to a horrible crescendo, then stopped, then started low and built up again . . . and again! It was in the *house* with me! It was the awful monster Buck Rogers had been fighting! It was the same frightful noise and it was *right down the hall* from me! It scared the living BEEJEESUS out of me! I was only about six or seven, but I wouldn't be at all surprised to learn that that was when my hair started to turn white.

Well, it turned out that Mom had been in a hurry and had left the upstairs phone off the hook when she went out. In those days, the diaphragm in the earpiece that made sound was a steel disk about the size of a fifty-cent piece. It could handle plenty of electricity. *Plenty*. Certainly enough to produce this fantastic horrible screeching—a noise so horrible I guess, that *nobody* could long bear it and somebody would quickly come search out whatever phone was making this god-awful sound and hang it up correctly, thus restoring order to the telephone company's world. And you can bet it worked! It was like an instant earache!

Ah, yes. "Ma Bell"—a sometimes not-so-benevolent despot of a mama if ever there was one.

Now, about Dr. Huer. I found out later, years later, that the man who had played Dr. Huer on the radio was an actor named Edgar Stehle and that, wonder of wonders, he actually lived right in my hometown! (Not so amazing, really. We were only about fifteen miles from the city and you could leave your house, walk briskly down to the railroad station and just zip right in.) But here's the part that I really did find amazing: he lived on the street right below ours! He lived only about a block away! He lived right under my nose! I probably rode right past him on my bike many times. Dr. Huer himself!

But wait, that's not all . . .

After more years had passed and I was (sort of) a grown man, I attended a reception of some kind at the town art museum. I had gone with my mother, who was a trustee of the museum. Maybe she needed an escort. And who should she introduce me to but Edgar Stehle! I think she'd planned it for my benefit. (*Thank* you, Mom!) He was a little gnome of a man with a balding, egg-shaped head and sort of pop-eyes, and when he spoke, the voice that came out was the high, reedy voice of Dr. Huer. He *looked* like Dr. Huer, he *sounded* like Dr. Huer. This was no actor—it *was* Dr. Huer!

I was standing there, all dressed up in reception-type finery, drinking reception-type punch out of a little reception-type glass (the kind you can't get your finger out of in a hurry), having a conversation about Buck Rogers with Dr. Huer himself! It didn't last long and it did bother me a little that he spoke of the radio show as if it had been long ago, but after all, it really had. He was from the twenty-fifth century and I probably bored him, but for me it was an incredible, wonderful, beautiful experience. I treasure it.

I also have some indelible memories of a few shows that must have come on around eight or nine at night. The sound, for instance, of a coin being dropped into drug store scale (*Ka-ching, ka-ching!* Those scales would spit out a little card with your weight and fortune printed on it) and the announcer saying slowly, ominously, "Weight: three hundred pounds. Fortune: DANGER!" It was "The Fatman!" (a tongue-in-cheek parody of the famous "Thinman," but I was too young to get the joke). All I remember is the fortune-telling scale and the Fatman's voice, which was deep and heavy. He sounded *big*.

Also there is a memory of "The Grand Canyon Suite" and the little weenie in the red jacket with brass buttons bawling "Cauuwllllll forrrr Pheeallleeip Moooorraaayis!" stuck in my head forever.

CHAPTER 16

Comic Book Heroes and Beachcombers

Well, yes, there were comic books, too. I can't say I was any sort of fanatic about them, though. I remember Superman and Batman, Captain Marvel, Captain America, Sub-Mariner, The Human Torch and Toro, Wonder Woman, The Green Lantern, The Blue Beetle, Plastic Man and even Donald Duck.

None of them were anywhere near as interesting as the radio shows. When I first saw Captain Midnight in a comic book, I was horrified.

"That's all wrong!" was my first thought. "That's *not* what he looks like!"

Because the simple artwork of a comic book could never come close to matching the images that I had built up in my mind over the years of listening to the radio. I was always disappointed by the sometimes downright badly drawn images in comic books. Imagination is so much better. That's another problem with T.V.

I was certainly no Superman fan. Ole Soupydoop just wasn't believable enough for me. With all those super powers, why wasn't he running the world? He certainly should have been able to take care of Hitler, Tojo, and Mussolini and end the war before suppertime any time he wanted to! Same goes for Captain Marvel.

Batman now, he was believable—almost. He could even bleed (though he did have an amazing recuperative ability, but then, they all did). I think the thing I liked most about Batman was the artwork. Bob Kane liked to do contrasty scenes with huge, looming shadows, perspective, depth, and dramatic effects. It made a lot of the other comics look like they had been drawn by six-year-olds. There was one issue with a villain in it called The Scarecrow that I've never been able to forget; the artwork really got to me. The title page showed a great, shadowy figure looming up from a dark field, filled with unforgettable menace. This guy was sure not about to dance away down any yellow-brick road with Dorothy and Toto! Not bad for a ten-cent comic book.

Batman's utility belt contained many amazing things, some of them possibly toxic chemicals, which you could imagine might cause him some embarrassment if they got loose in one of the scuffles he was always getting into. But anyhow, he seemed almost believable to me.

He was believable enough that you might even be tempted to try some of the things he did. He and his young companion, Robin, often swung on ropes across the streets far below—which, you have to admit, is quicker (and probably a lot more fun) than crossing in the normal way.

So of course, I tried it myself.

Well, it turns out that unless your rope is attached to a skyhook, as Batman's evidently was, it has to be attached to whatever it is you're trying to swing to. So, you can see what happens, right? You arrive at the end of your flight at whatever speed physics assigns you. No flaps, no dive brakes, no drag chute (unless you somehow used your cape), and your landing gear better be pretty robust! My own experiment involved about a twenty-foot rope, a tree branch, and another tree—and all I can say is, it is fortunate that young bones are "green" and bend easier than older ones.

Evidently you have to be a *very* gifted athlete to make it as a comic book character. Also you need to have a very strong grip. You need hands that snap shut like rattraps and hold like vices. It is not hard to launch yourself at a promising-looking branch. It's not even hard to hit it with both hands when you get there. But staying *attached* once your weight hits your hands—ah, *that's* what qualifies a true comic-book character or apprentice Ape-man!

Captain America seemed to be fairly human, too. At least bullets didn't bounce off him. But they did bounce off his shield, which he always seemed to be able to whip up in time to deflect them. I figured that shield must have been made of at least half-inch thick steel, maybe thicker. It had to be pretty heavy. Then one day, he had to cross the English Channel to get at some Nazis, so he slung it over his back and swam across, so fast that he churned up a lot of spray! That did it for me—Captain America was no longer believable.

But I did like Plastic Man. He was *so* weird. Donald Duck, too, oddly enough, was usually quite entertaining and interesting. He was always having outlandish adventures, like having a rocketship race to the moon with Baron DeSleezy and finding some moon people who said, "Foof, foof" and drank rocket fuel, or filling a sunken ship with ping pong balls to re-float it (a technique I think I recently saw being actually used by someone on TV—

seventy years later).

Many of the comic book characters did all their swinging from ropes and fighting with crooks while wearing a cape. Never could figure the cape out. Unless it made you invisible or was bulletproof, why would you wear a big piece of fabric that would get caught on things or trip you up, especially if your profession required you to engage in frequent street brawls?

I had a cape for a while. Mom made it for me out of a piece of red fabric. Best place to fly from was the top of Pop's bureau to the bed (this was *not* authorized by management—best to wait until Mom went out shopping). The cape was fine until the day I stepped on it during takeoff. I remember lying on the floor, staring at the ceiling, wondering if I was going to die before I started breathing again.

"WE INTERRUPT THIS PROGRAM TO BRING YOU A SPECIAL BULLETIN . . . "

Early on, after the big one on December 7, that phrase would freeze everyone in place and we all would "point" like dogs, attentively staring at the radio. Later on, the "special bulletins" sometimes got to be about as exciting as "drink Ovaltine" had been.

Lowell Thomas maybe, or John Gambling, would deliver the news in the cold, dark morning just before I had to get my galoshes and mittens on. The radio would be singing, "Ticonderoga pencils have won their way to fame, they're a fine American pencil, with a fine American name." And I would think, "No, mister, they are not. They are wood and yellow and too hard and the paint flakes off where your tooth marks are and they remind me of school. I want a neat mechanical pencil that I can carry in my back pocket along with my pen, in a holster, sort of like a six-gun! And so how did they 'win their way to fame,' anyhow? Did they get certificates and medals, like the Longines watches? ('Longines-Wittnauer: the world's *most honored* watch.') Is there a pencil museum somewhere? What's the story?"

Almost all announcers sounded alike: very puffed up with their own importance. All of them, that is, except Gabriel Heatter. (What did Gabe heat? And how?) Gabriel was different. Man, was he! Gabe would come on with the most *incredibly* overdone, lugubrious voice and say, "Awwww-ooooooohhhhhhh . . . there's *baaaaad* news tonight!" and at first you'd just freeze and think something like, "Oh no. *Oh no!* They've sunk the rest of our fleet!" or "They've done it. They bombed Washington and killed Frank!"

But his horrible news would turn out to be something relatively easy to take, like needing even more ration stamps when you went to buy a steak. (Ha! *Nobody* was eating steak much in those days! At least not that came from a cow.)

After a while, you got pretty used to the way Gabe came on, and he became a joke so easy to mimic that even *that* quickly grew old and it simply became boring. Of course, he could never tell us the *really* bad news, the truly horrible disasters that were happening regularly to us and our allies, because he didn't know about them. The government was keeping quiet about a lot of things because they were so depressing (and embarrassing).

Submarines, for instance, for the first half of 1942, were picking off our ships nightly, all up and down the east coast. The freighters and tankers were silhouetted against the bright lights of the cities along the coast, and early on they went down like ducks in a shooting gallery, sometimes as many as three in a night.

Nor could Gabe tell us that, for years, our own torpedoes were pretty much just expensive junk. The exploders didn't work. They would hit the target (our submariners would hear them go "clunk"), but not explode, and they often ran too deep. They would also explode prematurely from hitting the target's wake. This scandal caused the loss of many American lives and may have caused the war in the Pacific to last much longer than it needed to.

But they weren't about to let Gabriel Heatter, or any other newsmonger, know. And you can bet that when these things were finally being revealed after the war, many admirals were extremely uncomfortable about having any of it *ever* made public! They all got promoted, too. (On the other side of the Atlantic, the German torpedo designers who produced failures went to concentration camps.)

The great flood of sinkings along the coast naturally generated a whole lot of stories. The rumors were numerous and amazing! Of course, these are the kinds of incredible stories kids love to tell each other. Like the one your buddy heard about a kid who has a friend who lives down at the shore, and how he saw all these bodies washed up on the beach. Or the one about the cavalry horses who swam ashore from a torpedoed ship and were running all over the beach. Or the crates full of hand grenades, or the C-rations and life rafts and tons and tons of other neat stuff. Or how you could get pistols and knives off the bodies of sailors.

It is a little hard to sort this all out. In my recollection, most of us had a very healthy and highly developed fund of cynicism about these stories. "Aww, that's just a crazy rumor," we would tell each other. But that may have been jealousy speaking. Deep down, I think many of us *wanted* to believe, and many of the stories I now think, amazingly, had some sort of crazy truth in them, as perhaps many rumors do.

Bodies did indeed wash up on the beach, and I'm sure some of them did have knives on their belts, and I suppose some ghouls did rifle the bodies—of course it happened. But soldiers in full combat gear? I doubt it. But you never know. Someone in a panic may have given a foolish order. They might have had life jackets on, and some might have made it to the beach. But I don't think that a helmet, a pistol, a bayonet and a web belt full of cartridges would help you float much. I don't think, once you were in the water, that you'd want to keep much of that stuff on—or your combat boots, either.

Now, as for the horses. Ship loads of horses swimming ashore and running all over the beach? No, I don't think so. *Hoof prints* from horses all over the beach? Sure! Once you know that many of the shore patrols used horses to ride endlessly up and down the empty miles of beach, you can quickly see where that one came from! You could get a clue.

Cases of hand grenades? Doubt it. Seems like they would sink real quick. You never know, though; some cases might have been designed to float, I guess. Cases of C-rations, all still perfectly good because of their waxed waterproof cartons? Certainly. Chocolate bars that never melted? Sure—that was a D-ration. They were designed for the tropics and were half paraffin. (They weren't like any Hershey bar you've ever tasted, though. I bought one once in a surplus store; it was like biting into a stick.) Life Rafts? Well, what do you think? Of course. Do life rafts have all sorts of neat stuff, like signaling mirrors and flares and dye and little one-shot pistols and maybe even little hand-crank radios stashed on them? You betcha they do.

But on the other hand—on the *other* hand—let me ask you, let's consider: were you *allowed* to be out on most of those beaches? No, you weren't. Was it unlawful to pick up stuff you found on the beach stamped, "U.S."? What do you think? Had there been occasions when various theoretically loyal U.S. citizens had been known to actually row out to sea at night with their rowboats stuffed chockablock full of canned goodies and other trinkets, which they actually gave to surfaced U-boats? Yes there were. Right down there, just south of Seaside Heights lived at least one of them, as a matter of fact. Is Woody Allen's story about a friend who, while strolling on the beach near Coney Island one evening, saw a German U-boat surface right in front of his horrified eyes, true? Yes, indeed. It was unintentional and shocked everybody involved, both German and American, but it evidently did happen. The water there is not very deep and someone must have been a little off on the depth controls. What the sub did is called "broaching." *Scheisse!*

(Great Scott, but that must have been funny. Just imagine the torrents of polysyllabic German curses! Oh, the profanity!)

I have read that U-boats actually penetrated every single shipping harbor on the east and gulf coasts of the United States at one time or another.

Could you be taken for a possible spy if you were found poking around in the tide's latest delivery of flotsam? Yup. Shore could. Could you get shot?

Well . . . if you were apprehended and "run in," I'm pretty sure it would have been a lot more unpleasant than being "sent to the principal," for instance. A *lot* more. But they wouldn't have shot you. Not legally, anyway.

On the *other* hand, let's remember what we're talking about here. You're not up against what you'd call a mature, calm, reasonable, adult representative of the law. No, in reality the patrolman is probably just another kid—a big kid in a Coast Guard uniform but possibly even still in his teens. He has been given his own *horse* to ride (Yup. Just like you know who.) and a *loaded rifle*, and he has a license to shoot at anyone who runs. He is very bored, but he may be somewhat edgy, too, and when he spots you in the misty dark, he is probably spooked and full of adrenalin. Now, what do you think he's apt to do?

And probably you *would* try to run, too—right up to the dunes, and then back to wherever you lived, or your car—but you'd be pretty easy to track in wet sand. I'll bet the only thing that saved some people from getting shot was that the horse was jumpy because it had been spooked, too.

But never mind the danger. I'm sure that just added to the thrills! I'll bet my decoder badge that plenty of people, and not just kids either, went on midnight scavenger hunts out on the beach. I'll bet they got some neat stuff, too!

If I'd lived there, I would have done it. In any event, it must have been a lot of fun to live down there at the shore in those days. Exciting!

CHAPTER 17

String Beans and Peaches

Mom could be tough. She was a trim, compact redhead, and she could be scrappy. She was very big on patriotism, bravery, and stoicism. Particularly the last one. So was my father.

"Be a man!" my brother and I were often told, by both parents.

"But I'm just a little kid," I'd think. "How can I be a man yet? This is absurd."

You'd get told to "be a man" when you crashed your tricycle and skinned your knee (and there it is again, the knowledge of the coming Iodine burn). And we'd get told to "be a man" about other odd events, like when you had a cold and had coughed something up and needed to spit. "Swallow it like a man," Mom would say.

"Swallow it like a man?" Great Scott!

A *real man* would have hocked it up and spat it *SPLAT*, right on the floor. Or maybe in his hand and then wiped it on his pants—or no, by God, on his *shirt*!

But you didn't say that to Mom. No, no—that would have meant trouble. *Big* trouble.

Other times you'd get told to "be a man" about various foodstuffs. There might be some tears concerning spinach, for instance, or string beans. I really hate spinach, but my brother had a particular problem with string beans.

In all fairness, they were awful. During WWII, you only got canned string beans (perhaps even preserved by your own mother), which were greyish-green. And whether they had strings or not (and I think they did), they *sounded* like they did and they were a big problem. (It was about fifty years before I found out that the right cook can actually make string beans taste pretty good . . . almost.)

We got really adept at the art of making string beans disappear quickly whenever our parents went into the kitchen or weren't looking for some reason. On the windowsills, behind the curtains, on the cross bar of the table, in the grandfather clock, in the bookcase—mummified string beans were found in strange places all around the dining room area for decades after. I remember one piano-tuner man who . . .

Anyhow, to help my brother with his problem, my father came up with a diabolically clever plan to get him to eat his string beans. He'd load a fork with string beans and he'd tell Pete they were "Japs." Then he'd make a noise like an airplane and fly his forkful of "Japs" at Pete's mouth, the idea being that they'd go in and Pete would eat his "Japs," thus furthering the war effort! I thought it was nutty from the beginning. First off, who would want to eat a planeload of Japs, anyhow? Secondly, wouldn't that be illegal? But I kept my mouth shut, hoping for another episode of "fun with string beans."

I would watch, fascinated, as the great production developed:

"Now, you're gonna eat your Japs, ready? Here we go! *RRROOOOM, room, rooom!*" (Pete's lower lip would come out.) "*Rrrrooom, rooom, eeeeeyeeeooooaaaaaw!*" (Fork would approach mouth.) Pete would wait until the last second, then suddenly turn his head away. The planeload of Japs would hit the mountain, the forkful of string beans would go down his bib onto the floor, my father would say "DAMMIT!" my mother would say "LLOYD!" and I would laugh until I cried. My father didn't like *that* either.

"Shut up, you!" he would snarl, and at that point I'd try *hard* to stop, but it was almost impossible. Again, it felt like I would burst.

Another extreme wartime hardship we had to face on the home front was canned peaches. They were stringy. You'd try to swallow a slice, and you'd feel it go down, and that stringy thing would tickle the back of your throat (right in the gag place), and you'd try *hard* not to gag (gagging was also not approved by management), but you might. You might go "Aruk!" and your eyes might fill with tears, because at that point it took a lot of control not to let things go any further and bork your whole bowl. And you would want to be rewarded, you know, for being so strong and manly. But the only reward was to be told to do it again! Oh, the cruelty!

Peaches were a bad deal. Worse yet, they were nearly impossible to hide. They were wet, you see, and would drip—very bad on wallpaper—giving nearly instantaneous evidence of foul play.

I had a particular trick I played on my brother with peaches. He would have been told that he *had* to eat at least one piece, and my father would be watching him closely to prevent any trickery. When Pete got to the most critical part, the swallow, I would look directly into his eyes and go "A-GAK!" and watch his eyes fill with tears as he desperately tried not to gag.

He has never forgiven me.

Chapter 18

Bicycles, Liver and Air Raid Wardens

A t school in those days, there were occasional mysteries. Sometimes someone unfamiliar would suddenly come into the classroom and whisper something to the teacher, but we never were told what it was. Other times we could be out on the playground and have some interesting aircraft fly over, perhaps quite low, but if you missed a fly ball or worse yet, simply ignored it because you were watching airplanes, you were not likely to be asked to be on anybody's team after that.

There exists a class picture in which the whole damn class is standing on the school front steps looking at the camera except me. I'm looking at an airplane that was going over.

But the most interesting events happened outside of school.

In February 1942, the R.P. *Resor* was torpedoed only twenty miles off Mantoloking Inlet. A famous photograph of the tanker, awash amidships, burning and broken, was taken. The ship made a huge plume of black smoke, and I went up on the cliff to try to see it. I didn't see anything as I recall, and now, having done my map work, I realize I was not looking anywhere near far enough to the south, and it was over the curve of the earth from me anyhow. I'm sure it was visible from Point Pleasant and Seaside Heights, though, maybe even Atlantic City.

But I think I may have given the wrong impression about the beach. "Normal" people, people like you and me, couldn't just go to the beach—or "down to the shore" as we said in North Jersey (or as they say in Baltimore, "downeeuwchin, Hon")—like we do now. You could only do that if you actually lived there. There were normally so many patrols and soldiers that you could hardly even get close enough to *see* the beach, let alone walk on it! So much for picking up C-rations. And you couldn't just hop in the car and drive on down to the shore anyhow, under any circumstances. You could hardly hop in the car and go anywhere without careful planning, matter of fact—there just wasn't any gas to do it with. Gasoline was rationed, and if you didn't have the ration stamps and the right sticker on your car, you couldn't get more of it, no way, no how, no matter *how* much money you had! That was the theory, anyhow.

A reliable car, in working condition, was a hugely valuable thing. If you wore a tire out, or anything else, you weren't going to get a new one. Evah! Or at least not before the war ended. In 1942 that looked like it wasn't gonna be any time soon. Retreads were "in."

Well, yeah, there was something called the black market. People spoke of it with intense scorn. When people spoke of "war profiteers," they sometimes got a slightly wolfish look in their eyes, like maybe they felt like licking their lips (as the townspeople might have done back about six hundred years ago, thinking of burning some neighbor they didn't like at the stake).

But sometimes, if someone knew the right person, had some sort of a "contact," things could be done. Of course, that meant doing a forbidden thing, thus becoming a criminal. Even worse, it was unpatriotic! My father would not have dreamed of doing such a thing. Mom, now . . . I dunno. It's possible she might have pulled off a small crafty maneuver here or there concerning ration stamps, to "put a decent meal on the table." I dunno. I do know that I ate liver fairly often for lunch. That may have been for the sake of the iron in it.

Funny thing—and I never noticed (she confessed this to me years later)—she was never around when I was eating liver. She was always busy in the kitchen. Turns out she couldn't stand the thought of eating liver! It made her sick to think of it! She couldn't even look at it while cooking it; it "made her gag." So she would go hide in the kitchen while I ate. I never suspected.

Knowing that she did that makes it special. In fact, she giggled a little, like a naughty little girl when she confessed to me. She'd gotten away with it!

Actually, I kind of like liver to this day, but it has to be so well done that it's like shoe leather: "Just like Mom used to make." That said, I did once hear someone say, "What you're doing is eating the oil filter," and since then my intake of liver has fallen off some.

Early in the war we all got bicycles. I suppose it was to save on gasoline, and it certainly helped with the trip to school. My father took to riding his to work, which was about three miles away. I think he enjoyed doing it, at least on days with good weather, and it seems he started playing a game with himself called "get all the way to the office, no hands." Evidently he was able to do it, too, and that's no mean achievement, because there were some fairly steep grades on the route. But some busybody acquaintance of my mother's saw him going down Bradford avenue with arms folded one day and tattled on him to Mom, and then the fun ended and he had to promise not to do it any more.

One time while riding my bike along a sidewalk, I found a long wooden stick pole and decided to use it as a lance. I targeted one of those big mailboxes that extends all the way down to the sidewalk on four legs. I rode toward it with my lance held firmly beneath my right arm, hit it squarely (I was holding on tightly, I don't know what I was thinking, maybe to knock the big steel box over?) and found myself lying on my back, staring up at some bright, whirling little curlicues of light and then some branches and leaves.

Once again, it was impossible to breathe. One of the worst things about such uncomfortable moments, I found, was that they were apt to attract compassionate, well-meaning older women who thought you should be taken to a hospital immediately. One of these had evidently been driving by in her car and witnessed the whole thing. She stopped, got out, and stood over me, wringing her hands and warbling, "Ooh, ooh, ooh, little boy. Little boy, are you all right?"

Ugh! Ugh!

"Oh! Oh my! Little boy, are you hurt?"

I thought, *Lady, go away, leave me alone for God's sake, don't make a SCENE*, for I could not make a sound.

"Ooh little boy! *Speak* to me! What's the matter with you? *Say* something. Can't you *speak?*"

Lady just go away. Leave me ALONE!

"*Say* something, little boy! Can't you say *anything?*"

Well, what the hell do you think, lady? Don't you think if I could say something, I would? Just GO AWAY. Get AWAY from me. DON'T ATTRACT ATTENTION!

The paralysis was slowly starting to leave me, and I began to make some noises: "Ugh. Ugh. *Aarrrum.* Heeeeep."

"Little boy, are you all right? Can you talk?"

"Unnngh. Heeeeeep. Yeah. I'm O.K."

So I got up on my bike again and rode away—wobbly but as fast as I could—to get away from her and the scene of my huge embarrassment, leaving, I suppose, a somewhat frustrated and bewildered Florence

Nightingale behind me.

My own mother would, I think, have watched me for a while, just to make sure, then driven off with a bemused smile on her face, perhaps shaking her head a little.

Sometime during the first year of the war my father volunteered to be an air raid warden. Every neighborhood had to have one, I think it was for only one street. He had a special white helmet that was shaped like a WWI doughboy helmet and that had a special Civil Defense insignia on the front. He might have carried a flashlight and a whistle, too. His duty was to go up and down the street, checking to see if anyone was showing any light from behind their blackout curtains. He had a lot of trouble with our next-door neighbor, Mrs. Waldron. She evidently felt that the whole thing was just a silly game and didn't take it very seriously. Lights were always showing around the Waldron house, and she and my father went round and round. I think the whole exercise was only followed during air raid drills.

My friend Louise's mother volunteered to be an air raid warden too. *Her mother?* Yes, her *mother*, for God's sake, alone out there in the dark, doing a man's job! I bet she did a bang-up job of it, too, though Louise and her three sisters were somewhat horrified when they saw their mother getting all fitted out in her helmet and special vest, whistle, and flashlight, preparing to march out and shape up the neighbors.

Many women were delighted at having a chance to "do something."

Mac, another close buddy of mine, told me a story of his father and a neighbor, who, as air raid wardens, went down to the bottom of their street and threw stones at a lit streetlight, trying to knock it out. It was not a little gas lamp either; it was full-sized and electric. Grove Street was a county road and was probably not in their authorized area, anyhow.

Throwing stones to break a streetlight! That's the sort of vicious, criminal thing we used to do on "mischief night" before Halloween, and if the police saw you, you had better be light on your feet.

So, that's more or less what was going on in parts of North Jersey toward the end of 1942.

At Stalingrad the German soldiers were eating their horses.

1943

Chapter 19

Seen in the Sky

By 1943, the war news was beginning to sound better and better. Of course, we kids had always assumed we would win. The thought of losing the war just never entered our minds. But now we were starting to hear frequent news of victories. In February, the Germans surrendered at Stalingrad, and at Guadalcanal we found, to our surprise, that what we had thought to be Japanese reinforcements coming *in* had actually been ships taking troops *away*, and that the Japanese had completely abandoned the island.

Our First Marine Division, most of them sick with malaria, had been replaced there by army troops during the last days of 1942.

In November of that same year, American troops had landed all along the northeast coast of Africa. The Germans and Italians, led by the previously mentioned genius of armored warfare, Erwin Rommel, had been fighting the British back and forth across the northern coast of Africa since 1940. Now the Afrika Corps was caught between two fires, and after turning suddenly to give the Americans a very bloody nose at a place called Kasserine Pass, continued to retreat toward the last piece of Africa across from Sicily. So it began to look like we were winning on all fronts.

Bizerte is a town in Africa very near to where the final battles occurred. I remember that a song called "Dirty Gertie from Bizerte" briefly became popular.

Early in 1943, probably in January, there was a tremendous ice storm in North Jersey. Ice covered all the trees, and a lot of branches came down in the streets. There was some talk about staying home from school, but my parents, strong believers in stoicism and strength of character, weren't about to raise any summer soldier, so it was decided that I must go.

I walked to school because there were so many branches down that cars couldn't get around. I remember being fascinated by a fallen power line that was sparking and making a brilliant white little fire with lots of bluish smoke in the street. I knew better than to get too close to it.

When I got to the classroom, I found that I was the *only* boy in the third grade who had come to school that day; all the others had gotten off.

But there was one other boy in the class, a new kid I didn't know, who had evidently just moved. He seemed to always be smiling, with his eyes all crinkled up. But what really impressed me was that he was wearing a leather aviator's helmet. His name was Royce. Sometime around mid-morning, he needed to go to the boy's room, and since it was in the basement in a different part of the school and I was the only other boy in class that morning, I was detailed to show him where it was. Our friendship started then, and we've been very good friends ever since.

Years later, after we had all grown up, he married Louise.

I occasionally enjoy mentioning to him that I've known her longer than he has.

And that she kissed me first.

Some of the songs Americans were singing then were "Pistol Packing Mama" and "My Spurs Go Jingle, Jangle, Jingle." I think "Deep In the Heart of Texas" had come out earlier, because on a Christmas trip to D.C. to visit my father's parents, I remember my friendly, fun-loving Aunt Katherine trying to get me to clap my hands when the people in the song did. "C'mon, Jimmeh, clap yo' hans!" she would shout at me. (D.C. was considered a southern city then, and many of its residents spoke with somewhat southern accents.)

One afternoon—I think it was either in spring or summer—I was outside in front of our house when I heard a roaring sound approaching. The sky to the north, above the cliff, suddenly filled with airplanes heading east. They were brown and looked sort of short and stubby. They just kept on coming, rising up and down like birds. It seemed like a vast flock of them but was really probably about forty. I'd never seen anything like it. I am pretty sure now that what I was seeing was a sort of milestone in Air Force history, when Dave Schilling led his entire group of P-47s across the country to Teterboro airport in New Jersey to be loaded onto ships to take them to England.

Another time, also in the afternoon, my mother and I were out in front of the house and saw, up over the north cliff again, an extremely bright fireball flying west to east on what looked to be a horizontal trajectory. It didn't appear to be dropping at all; maybe it just skipped off and went back out into space. It didn't go amazingly fast; it just flew steadily all the way across the northern horizon.

It was really pretty spectacular. A blazing ball of white light with an orange glare around it. If it had happened at night it would have lit up the entire landscape.

I'm almost 100 percent sure it was just a big space rock paying a brief visit . . . almost.

My father belonged to the Lions Club, and one day the members of the club were invited to bring their sons along on a special trip they had arranged, to go see some of the airplanes that were being built for the air force. (At that time it was the United States *Army* Air Force, or USAAF.) There in the hanger, or maybe it was a showroom, were some brand-new fighter airplanes. Possibly there were others, but all I remember were the P-51 and the P-47. I was surprised to see them without paint. All the pictures I had ever seen of warplanes showed them in dappled coats of brown and green, or blue and gray for the navy. I had never seen an airplane without paint before. Another surprise was that the aluminum skins had not been outdoors yet and hadn't had any time to oxidize. I think they had been buffed, for the aircraft shone like mirrors.

The P-51 was a nice, businesslike-looking little aircraft, but at that time it had not yet had a chance to show what an all-time classic it would become. I think it was probably a P-51B, as it did not yet have the bubble canopy.

The big surprise to me was the P-47. It seemed gigantic! It loomed above the P-51 and really seemed too big to be called a fighter. This muscular aircraft weighed more than any other single-engine WWII fighter, but its big engine had the power to move it along as fast as anyone else—especially going downhill, which was something the pilots had to be careful about. It also carried more machine guns than anyone else, and those eight .50 calibers could do huge damage when strafing targets on the ground. Seeing it so bright and shiny seemed somehow wrong to me. In my mind, all Thunderbolts had to be brown, like the ones I had seen flying in that big group above the cliff, heading for Teterboro.

I don't really remember what we were doing in gym class in those days, but I think that running was considered somewhat important. That was when I realized that other people could run faster than I could. I couldn't understand how they could possibly move their legs so fast without falling on their faces.

My friend Royce was even then starting to show some signs of having possibly been created in a secret laboratory somewhere. He could run faster than anyone else, though Charlie Martin could give him a good race. But in any other sport, Royce was just about unbeatable, so I asked him to teach me how to run.

Well. He took hold of my hand and we started running. I thought I was going to get killed, but I had no choice; I had to move my legs fast enough to keep from falling on my face and probably leaving it behind on one of the big slate paving stones that made up the sidewalks of the town. Over the years most of them had been heaved up by tree roots, so they did not make for a smooth running surface. In the end, I lived through the experience, and we ran together several other times, with me trying mightily to keep up with him. I never could, but I did learn how to run faster. Later on that turned out to be useful on various soccer fields.

Some books and authors will tell you that 1942 was the year that doomed the Axis, but I think that it was in 1943 that we really began to know and feel it.

The war had gone on for so long that for kids around my age it was just an accepted way of life. We hadn't really been old enough when it began to remember anything else, and when the war started it made almost no difference to our lives at all, except that there were now some much more interesting things to think and talk about.

We accepted almost everything we were told about our evil enemies: that the Germans were extremely cold-blooded, brutal and pitiless, but sometimes dangerously clever, and that the Japs were even worse. The Japs were seen as small, vicious, not-quite-human animals, *always* treacherous, who liked to torture prisoners. Since they wouldn't surrender, it looked like we were going to have to kill them all, like you would do with rats or mosquitoes.

Well, O.K. then, let's do that.

What's the problem? Maybe you've forgotten how kids think.

The USAAF, which had been making heavier and heavier raids on various targets in Europe as it learned its trade, went to Germany for the first time in January. About fifty-five aircraft bombed Wilhelmshaven, and the German defenses were somewhat taken by surprise. It was not a huge blow to German industry or morale, but it did give a small hint of what was to come. We were determined to do "precision" bombing by daylight, and as time went on, we did score occasional impressive successes. A colonel named Curtis LeMay was responsible for some of those.

But more often, struggling with terrible flying weather in northern Europe, endless mechanical problems, and the steadily increasing effectiveness of the German defenses, the "precision" results were not successful.

As time went on, the air battles between the USAAF and the Luftwaffe became epic.

The British had tried daylight bombing earlier and had lost so many aircraft that they decided to bomb by night instead. Since finding one particular target, like a factory, was then virtually impossible at night, they developed a method of setting fire to the whole area surrounding the factory. That worked so well that it quickly grew into trying to burn up entire cities, just as the Germans had tried to do to the British in 1940.

Also in January, the British bombed Berlin for the first time since 1941. It was a much heavier raid than they had carried out before, as the RAF had been busy developing some larger, more capable four-engine bombers that could carry much bigger loads.

On the following night, the Germans bombed London in retaliation.

Most of my memories of the war in 1943 seem to involve *Life* magazine. We also got the *Saturday Evening Post*, and I would jump on that as soon as it arrived and eagerly go through it for the sake of the cartoons, as well as the airplane and sometimes battleship pictures. *Life* magazine was good, too. They printed some fine pictures; most that I remember were from the war in the Pacific and had to do with the great naval battles. One particularly dramatic shot I recall was of one of our carriers, the *Wasp*, listing a bit in the water with a huge, billowing cloud of smoke towering to one side above her—ominous evidence of an explosion in her hull.

There was no war in the European theater yet except for the air war. But there were some very interesting articles about that.

In the air, the British had been getting more effective all the time. In May they made the famous Dambuster Raid, when they tried to destroy three dams that supplied power to 75 percent of the Ruhr, Germany's main industrial region. It was an amazingly clever and skillful attack, successfully breaching two out of the three dams, but the Germans put a massive effort into the repair and had them back filling up again in three months—now much better protected.

In July, after a helpful period of hot, dry weather, the RAF went after the German city of Hamburg. Blinding enemy radar by releasing clouds of aluminum foil strips, 740 RAF bombers went over the city on the first night and sent down 2300 tons of incendiary and high explosive bombs. Twenty-three hundred *tons*. The fires were immense, but "Bomber" Harris was not done with Hamburg yet. After a two-day pause, during which the USAAF went to the city by day and bombed industrial targets, the RAF went back with their entire force again. This time conditions were just right and the bombing pattern was so concentrated that a rare phenomenon called a firestorm was created. There was no wind, so all the fires merged and the heat went straight up, creating a chimney-like effect in the atmosphere, which created hurricane-force winds on the surface, rushing in from all directions toward the fires.

Everything in the central fire area was destroyed. Returning bomber crews estimated that the column of fire had reached three miles high. The German leaders were badly shaken and Albert Speer, in charge of German war production, estimated that about six more such attacks would force Germany to give up. That was exactly what Bomber Harris was aiming for, and he kept on trying, but was only able to achieve the monstrous firestorm effect a few more times before the end of the war.

He sent the bombers back to Hamburg twice more on succeeding nights, but while the third raid was effective, no firestorm was created, and the fourth one was a near disaster for the attackers. Powerful thunderstorms descended all across northern Europe that night and badly scattered the bombers and their bombs. The fires that did start were made much easier to deal with by the torrents of rain that fell. Most of the RAF losses that night were caused by weather.

But Hamburg was a dead wasteland, and stories told by the shocked refugee survivors sent ripples of apprehension all across Germany.

They were indeed beginning to reap the whirlwind.

Chapter 20

Thunderstorms and Hooky

That summer there were some big thunderstorms in New Jersey, too. A spectacular one with huge black and purple rolling clouds was coming up from the south one afternoon, and I went up on a big rock mound across the street to watch it. I took along my grandfather's big black umbrella in case it started to rain. The clouds were impressive; they rolled and boiled up into the sky right over my head. It started to sprinkle a little, so I opened the umbrella and watched from under it. Suddenly I felt a buzzing electric shock in my hands. It wasn't as bad as sticking my finger into an electric light socket (which I did have personal experience with—I don't want to talk about it), but it was close. I felt the hair rise up on my neck and I carefully, slowly (so as not to attract the lightning's attention) shut the umbrella and stealthily, bending over, crept down off the rocks, feeling all the way like a small bug that was about to be squooshed by a gigantic hammer in the sky. I was really scared.

There had been a recent demonstration of lightning's power just across the street from us in the McKinneys' yard, when a tall tulip tree had been struck. I was in our living room at the time, so I was only about fifty feet away from it. The windows had been closed (I was surprised they didn't break), but the flash and thunderclap were instantaneous and shattering. I swear that I heard a sudden "Fzzzt!" just before the bolt struck, too.

After the storm passed, there was a great long strip of bark lying on the ground, about a foot wide, several inches thick, and easily thirty feet long in a spiral—like the curlicues of shavings that fall on the floor when you plane a board. In memory, I can still see the foot-wide cut in the side of the tree, shockingly white, extending from the ground all the way up the trunk where the bark was missing. It amazes me that it didn't kill the tree, but it didn't, and

111

that tree stood tall and proud for many more years.

I have no way of knowing how close I came to getting zapped when I was up under the umbrella, but I can tell you for sure that the Ben Franklin story is at least partially true. Clouds do have electricity in them!

I think we went to the Rhode Island coast again that same summer. My cousin Ted and I roomed together in the only room in the house that was above the first floor. From the window, we could see the whole expanse of the tidal pond on which the house was located, the little wooded island nearby, and all the way across a half-mile of water to the thin strip of sand that separated the pond from the ocean. The sand was just high enough to keep us from seeing the surf breaking on it.

We could row to the small island near the house in a rowboat, but once you were there, the only place to go was little slope of bare rock. The low, thickly tangled bushes were virtually impossible to get through. Not only that, but according to my cousins, there were both Germans *and* Japs on that island!

There was some anxiety about a hurricane that was grinding along offshore. After 1938, people in Rhode Island sat up and paid attention when they heard the word "hurricane," but it never came ashore. We awoke the next morning to an amazingly clean, clear atmosphere. Everything seemed to have sharp outlines, and the sea across the lagoon and beyond the far-away strip of beach was a deep, dark blue. We looked out the window as we were getting dressed and thought we saw something strange. There it was again! Something out there, on top of the sand, half a mile away, occasionally flashing white. We looked at the beach for a while, mystified, and then realized that what we were seeing were the tops of some very *big* waves crashing on the beach.

After breakfast, we all got in the motorboat and went across the water to the beach. The surf was spectacular. The huge waves had been created by the hurricane, which had passed by offshore. I don't think I have ever since personally experienced surf so large. The sand shook beneath our feet every time one of the big ones hit.

Something that fascinated me in those days was bullet shells. We couldn't have any guns, couldn't have any real bullets, and there were no caps for our cap guns, but empty shells—well that was something, anyhow. One day, while exploring down some sandy country road behind the beach, I found, to my great delight, several ancient, empty .22 caliber shells. They were right next to a fence post where the shooter had probably braced his rifle while he took a shot at a woodchuck or something. I was very excited and felt like I'd found treasure.

And while I was doing this, some kids my age in England were disassembling a real German bomber that had crashed in a forest, taking *real* working machine guns out of it, with belts of real *live bullets*, setting them up in a real fort in the woods, squeezing off a few rounds, and defying the authorities to come and get them!

Summer passed and I started fourth grade. Around this time, Royce and I decided to try playing hooky from school. I think we may have gotten the idea from some book, possibly *The Adventures of Tom Sawyer*, or maybe from one of the boy's magazines Royce got. We wanted to try it just so we could say we had done it and to find out what it was like. I don't remember the early details of our escape; I imagine we just walked away after lunch when we were supposed to be out on the playground. Then we would have gone down a side street away from the school and away from Lorraine Avenue, which led up to the town center. Then we'd have crossed Valley Road, maybe up by Mountainside Park, and then up the slope of the first Watchung and into the woods.

Then I would have felt secure, for that was my territory.

I think we had read about going down to "the old swimming hole" when playing hooky. It was mandatory. Only there wasn't any swimming hole. The only open water anywhere nearby was a reservoir, and it was surrounded by a barbed-wire fence. We went down through the woods about a mile and checked it out. Those barbed-wire fences were never any problem to near-monkeys like us who liked to climb. Our hands were small enough to grab the wire between the barbs and the toes of our shoes fit into the diamond-shaped spaces between the fence wires like steps of a ladder. *Hup, hup, one, two, three, hoop-la!* And we would be over the fence and in. All you had to do was move slowly and carefully as you went over the top, being careful to not get snagged on anything.

The woods inside the fence were different. There were some pines, I think, and the land around the edge of the reservoir was untouched by human activity. It seemed clean. There were a few trees, but it was not thickly wooded. I think there may have been a lining of flat rocks where the edge sloped down into the water. We gingerly crept down to the edge and felt the water. It was *cold* . . . and Royce wanted to go swimming!

Away across the long expanse of water there was a cube-shaped stone building, about two stories high. It had something to do with the reservoir, maybe control of the flow of water in and out. If there were anyone in it, they probably weren't looking out at the unchanging view, but if they had been, two young naked boys illegally splashing about in the water across the way would have instantly attracted attention.

Aside from that, I have to admit, I didn't really *want* to take my clothes off and get wet and cold. As a matter of fact, I have *never* liked to do that. So at that point, I chickened out, and we retreated. We went back over the fence, bunnied quickly across the road (though nobody would have cared if they had seen us), and darted up into the woods, following a stream I knew about. I was trying to find a pool or something for Royce to swim in; I knew it was an important part of the hooky experience for him. But all we could find was a wide place in the stream about two feet wide and four feet long. It might have been a foot deep. So we got down to our underwear and splashed about a little, but this water was also plenty cold and the sun was mostly hidden behind the trees.

O.K., now what do we do? We didn't know what time it was (during the war it was a rare kid who had a watch), and showing up at home too early would have raised some uncomfortable questions. But I probably knew enough about the late afternoon shadows on the cliffs down where we lived to know that it was safe to appear.

So that was our first great hooky adventure. I think we both had a slight feeling of letdown. It hadn't been all that exciting.

And yet, when you look at it objectively, our day had been one that any sensible educator ought to applaud. We'd had a good adventure, all of it outdoors (healthy) in bright sunlight (Vitamin D) in the clean, clear air (true, it was North Jersey in 1943, with what you'd call an industrial atmosphere, but you'd only smell it now and then, when the wind was in the east). We'd been physically active, running and climbing over barbed wire, almost like real infiltrators (good training), and by choice had done a lot of things that a bunch of slightly older kids dressed in khaki were being told to do that afternoon only a few miles south of us down at Fort Monmouth or Camp Dix.

I am sure it was better for us than being indoors all day, trying to remember what Abner Van Yocum said to Baron Von Buren about the treaty of Bhent or what nine times five is.

That said, I probably learned a lot of useful things in third grade, but the major thing I still remember (and my teacher was another kid who was even more of an airplane freak than I) was how to draw the canopy and very difficult rudder on a Spitfire.

Thanks to Royce, I also came out of it able to run a lot faster than when I went in.

CHAPTER 21

Invasions Good and Bad

In July, the Allies invaded Sicily, but all I remember about it is that we followed the progress of the armies, which turned into something of a race, with the British trying to fight their way north along the island's eastern coast and the American army under General Patton going first west, then north, circumnavigating the island, and coming back toward the east in an unplanned and surprising end run. The Germans defended themselves strongly against the British under Montgomery, but they sort of left the back door open and Patton just about beat the British to the strait of Messina, the narrow channel of water between Sicily and Italy where the monsters Scylla and Charybdis were supposed to live.

If the Allies had been able or quick enough, they might have taken advantage of a great opportunity to attack the Germans as they tried to escape across the strait, but the opportunity was fumbled and lost. Perhaps there just weren't enough nearby airfields yet.

That summer there was a big uproar over a book titled *Generation of Vipers* by an author named Philip Wylie. The book bad-mouthed all sorts of American icons, such as Mom, Momism, the Boy Scouts, the PTA, baseball, etc., and it caused a huge stink. Some people thought Phil Wylie was in league with the devil and that he should be tarred and feathered, but others thought he was pretty clever and enjoyed seeing the great symbols of "the American way of life" take a few hits. All in all, it was a great big flap.

I've never read the book, but I have read some of his science fiction stories, which I thought were very good. It turned out that my mother had known Phil Wylie in school and I thought her only comment on the affair was quite intriguing.

"He was a *horrible* little boy," she said.

Toward the end of the year, we invaded the atoll of Tarawa in the Pacific. The little island was smaller than Central Park in New York City. Largely due to our ignorance about the tides in the lagoon and because the brass hats ignored the warnings of the one man who had personal experience of them, our marines had to wade for thousands of feet under fire, sometimes in chest-deep water (which soon turned red), before getting to the beach. The battle cost us about a thousand dead marines and several thousand more wounded. Not only that, but one of our carriers in the invasion fleet was sunk by an enemy submarine, costing an additional loss of seven hundred sailors.

There had been almost five thousand Japanese on the island, and sure enough, they wouldn't surrender. They kept on fighting until almost all of them were dead, and we took only about twenty prisoners, most of whom were probably wounded and unable to resist when taken.

This made the idea of island hopping all the way to Japan look pretty grim.

The USAAF, which had made its first raid on Germany with fifty-five planes in January, had fought many huge, bitter air battles with the Luftwaffe during 1943—battles that made the Battle of Britain look like a preliminary bout. The 8th Air Force had suffered great losses, but during the year, it had grown some and was able to end 1943 with a raid by 710 bombers on Kiel.

The inexorable growth continued and by the end of the next year it would take an entire hour for the bomber stream to pass over a given point. But the vast torrent of bombs just drove German industry underground, where it continued to function. After the war, many people had the opinion that perhaps the bombing effort had been wasted.

There is no doubt however, that the Germans used the equivalent of an entire army plus 80,000 high-velocity cannons for air defense at home. That might have been enough to make a big difference on the Russian front, perhaps even altering the outcome of the entire war.

1944

CHAPTER 22

A New Year

As a special treat on New Year's Eve, my brother and I were allowed to stay up past midnight. The late bedtime was exciting, and it was particularly exciting to hear the celebration as people rang in the New Year. The sounds now are so puny compared to past New Years' celebrations that it's pitiful.

Of course there were air-raid sirens then (lots of them), but there were also big factory steam whistles and train whistles and even some boat whistles, too. Not only that, but I think almost everyone who owned a car leaned on the horn for at least a minute. The cumulative sound was amazing.

The air-raid sirens did lend a special note to it, though, they surely did.

Perhaps, since we were at war, it was a relief to relax a bit and blow off steam by making a lot of noise. Almost everyone was working hard and not getting enough sleep. The war, while no longer a real source of fear for Americans (except for those with close relatives in uniform), was *the major fact of life*, always lurking in the background, coloring everyone's thoughts. Everything else was secondary.

We didn't worry much about the Japanese on the East Coast, but on the West Coast they still lived with the possibility of Japanese air raids and surprise attacks all the time.

The news and pictures of the carnage at Tarawa were just beginning to filter back and be digested by the American public. It was the first time that such comprehensive coverage and explicit photographs of dead American servicemen had been allowed in the States. It caused a shudder of revulsion to run through the country as people began to appreciate the true eventual size of the butcher's bill they were just beginning to pay. By this time, almost everyone had a relative or friend who was in the military.

119

On the East Coast, I think we were getting somewhat complacent. We certainly weren't worried about being invaded by the Germans; they had their hands full in Russia, where they were gradually beginning to lose ground. German U-boats, which had been such a tremendous threat earlier in the war, were now the hunted instead of the hunters.

So perhaps the wonderful outpouring of sound that I remember from New Years' Eves during the war years was, by that time, partly the sound of triumph. We knew we had faced and were fighting a monstrous enemy and that we were finally winning.

Maybe it was just fun to make a lot of noise for a change.

The only specific celebrations that have stayed in my memory are the ones we had down the street at the Wells' house. Mr. and Mrs. Wells would have gone out to a party and the four of us kids—Ronny, Gary, my brother, and I—would have the big old house to ourselves. I don't recall that we did much while we waited for midnight—maybe listened some to the radio babbling about Times Square.

There would be some very big pieces of hard coal smoldering on the grate in the fireplace. I remember being surprised to see a penny we had put in among the coals turn red-hot within just a minute or two.

"Hey! Quit putting on more coal—don'tcha know there's a war on?"

We'd check the clock almost every minute as the magic hour neared, maybe suiting up in our winter coats (Navy pea jackets were popular), then taking them off again because we'd gotten too hot—definitely antsy. Then it would finally be time, and we'd rush out on the big porch to make our small noises and listen, amazed, to the big one.

First a few solitary car horns—early birds jumping the gun. We'd beat on some pans and whistle, maybe yell "Happy New Year!" a few times, but then we'd hear it coming, and we'd fall silent.

The sound would rise up from the land, all across the plain between us and the big city on the horizon. It would build slowly: a thousand—or maybe a hundred thousand—voices echoing from the distance, building and building, closer, bigger, nearer, rising up until it seemed like a huge wind of sound. I would stand there in the frosty darkness, struck dumb, listening in awe while the vast wail of thousands of factory whistles, horns, bells, and hundreds upon hundreds of air-raid sirens in full cry around us rose up to the stars.

That was an amazing sound. It really was. I hope someone somewhere recorded it, for we will never hear its like again. I doubt that factories have steam whistles any more, and there are now very few air raids. For a few years after the war, they would sound the sirens for a minute at noontime on weekends to see if they still worked, but even that soon ended.

New Years' celebrations in North Jersey during WWII—I feel sorry for those who don't know, never heard, and can't imagine what that sound was like.

Another thing I remember doing at the Wells' house was helping cars get up Bradford Avenue in the snow. I am not sure why we were there after dark—it may be that it was early on New Year's Eve—but I know that we did this more than once. Maybe double wartime savings time had something to do with it, because the sun seemed to go down at about 3:30.

If it had snowed, we could hear from the house all sorts of sounds indicating various degrees of a car's success or failure to make it up the hill. During the war, car tires were apt to be old and getting somewhat bald. Often, as a car got to the part of the road that curved uphill, they'd lose traction and we'd hear that magic sound:

Rum-rum-veeEEEEEOOOooo-rum-rum-veeEEEEEOOOooo-rum-rum-rum-veeeEEEEE—

You know. And frequently we would put our jackets on and go out and help the driver out, pushing the car until it got traction again. It was fun, actually—gave you a feeling of accomplishment, maybe a hidden feeling that "Well, *that* ought to cancel out some of the black marks I've gotten." Because we all had records that were not entirely what you'd call "clean." Like that time you threw that snowball through that garage window, for instance.

There was another sound you were sure to hear sooner or later when it had snowed: *Wip-wip-wip-wip-wop-wop-WAP-WAP-WAP-WAP-wop-wop-wop-wop-wop-wop* . . . And passing away into the distance—an inescapable curse riding along with someone, because it meant that they had a broken chain. Which meant that if they didn't stop pretty soon and remove it, it was going to bash holes in their wheel well, which would soon rust out. There was no way to replace that part; they'd either have to have it fixed up in a welding shop, or just let it fall off and ride around in what had become a junker.

Chains came in twos: two chains side by side, about three inches apart, connected with hard pieces top and bottom and a strap that went through an opening in the rim of the wheel. You'd pass the strap through the opening and through a clamp at the other end of the chains and clamp it down tight. That was very important, getting them tight. If you didn't, then you were apt to hear *wap-wap-wap* coming from the back of the car much sooner than otherwise. If you weren't lazy, you'd start to put three of these assemblies on each tire, but by the time you got to number six, you'd be real tired of the whole exercise, say the hell with it, and live with two.

Putting chains on when it was a cold, gloomy, wet morning was a very nasty job. You had to squat, because if you knelt, you'd get your pants wet on the knee. The chains would be cold and messy, and you had to reach up into the wet, dirty wheel well to get the strap around from in back and through the slot (impossible to do without getting your sleeve wet and muddy). All told, it was a really bad way for a working man to start the day.

What was even worse was that our driveway sloped upward to the street. When it snowed, you almost had to have chains on to make it out. The road would probably have snow on it too, as it was not heavily traveled. But then you'd get to streets with more traffic, and those might have been plowed down to bare pavement. At any rate, you were apt to drive on bare pavement somewhere, sooner or later. Then you had another problem. The chains liked snow; they were designed for it. But they did not like bare pavement, or the pavement didn't like chains. If you drove with them on bare pavement for long enough, ok they would surely break. Then, you know. *Wap-wap-wap-wap-wap* . . . beating the hell out of your wheel well. You'd *have* to stop and take off the broken one.

My father really hated chains.

Sometimes on cold winter nights, we'd hear a "Phantom Bagpiper." We would hear him late at night up in the quarry, which gave his music an echo, making a weird sound even weirder. The strange, wailing serenade would go on for half an hour or so. I actually kind of enjoyed it. Mom would sometimes ask me if I'd seen anybody, and my answer was always no. But of course I was not about to get out of my warm bed and go out there in the cold to look. Sometimes after it was over, I did hear footsteps going down the road, creaking on the snow, but I never did see anyone. I prefer to believe it was a spirit.

Another apparition we would often witness was a man we called "Crazy Jed." Jed rode a horse, which memory tells me was white, though it might have been gray, and he would come up the street, headed for the quarry and who knows where after that. You'd sometimes see him riding along the streets lower down in town, too.

The Wells brothers gave him his name. I don't know why they called him "crazy"—probably just because he rode a horse around. Nobody else did this; thus he was crazy. Why "Jed"? I don't know that either. There was a character on the radio called "Tennessee Jed" who was supposed to be a crack shot, though. That's probably where it came from.

No doubt this winter was another very cold one, for I remember hearing the phantom bagpiper's footsteps squeaking on the snow as he went down the street.

CHAPTER 23

Trophies

In school in 1944 we were making up Red Cross packages for prisoners of war. We would bring things like bars of soap, pairs of socks, razor blades, and needles and thread to be put in them. Each box was about the size of a shoebox.

My father had some sort of secret job at the time. He was very cagey about it, and I am pretty sure he greatly enjoyed letting us know that he couldn't tell us anything about what he did, that it was a *military secret*. After the war, he was able to tell us that he had been working on camouflage plans for factories.

I think that job enabled him to get a "B" sticker for the rear window of his car, which authorized him to get more gasoline than the normal citizen could, because he was in a defense specialty. I bragged about it to some friends, which was a mistake, because when the special job ended, he, being the upstanding, honest, ultra-patriotic citizen that he was, scraped the sticker off and went back to being a normal, boring "A" sticker person. I have since taken some gas about my bragging from those friends.

He had also been one of the architects who worked on the design of the observation tower at the top of the Empire State Building in New York. Several times, I heard him poo-pooh, with great scorn, the legend that there had ever been a plan to moor dirigibles to it.

The movies were a favorite pastime in those days. When we went to the movies, there would sometimes be a double feature, and that didn't just mean two full-length movies; it also meant "News of the Week," previews of coming attractions, maybe a short on some patriotic subject, and, if we were lucky, several cartoons. I would often come out of the theater with a headache and maybe feeling a little "icky in the garden" from eating too many Good 'n' Plenty's or Ju-Ju Bees.

I think each show began with the playing of the national anthem. I remember various scenes of West Point being shown while it played. Early in the war I believe we all stood at attention in the theater with our hands over our hearts during the anthem, but I don't think that lasted to the end of the war. Seems to me the price of admission for a kid was about twenty-five cents, maybe less. I have a snapshot memory of clenching two dimes in my sweaty paws, waiting for the line to move.

During the Christmas season, probably on the weekend, the movie theater would screen a special Christmas show that started, I think, around noon and lasted for a *long* time. They would have at least two features and an incredible number of cartoons and all sorts of other special short features for a remarkably low price. The line for those events would extend across the road and all the way up the hill of Bellevue Avenue.

In Europe, the 8th Air Force had begun bombing what were called "crossbow sites" in France. Nobody was quite sure what they were for, but they were shaped like skis and all seemed to point toward London. Only a few Generals, politicians and intelligence people knew that they were somehow connected with a very ominous-sounding robotic flying bomb project the Germans had been developing.

The build-up to the invasion of Europe had been going on in England for a long time, but now the island seemed like it was about to burst. In addition to all the soldiers from the British Commonwealth, there were now about two million American service people (which the British felt was more than enough!). Everyone knew the invasion was coming, but nobody had a good idea of when it would be, so naturally, all sorts of theories and rumors were floating about.

I think that rationing started to ease up around this time, too. More and more things were now available without ration stamps. But we still frequently ate cheese soufflé and spaghetti casserole.

That was a meal I really liked, that casserole. It was many years before I found out that "casserole" is a sort of generic term and that there are other kinds of casseroles, too. Mom made the dish with spaghetti and some ground hamburger, some pieces of green pepper (I think), mushrooms, onion, and pieces of tomato. The tomatoes had been canned or preserved (maybe by Mom), and small pieces of tomato skin would also end up in the casserole, rolled up to about the diameter of a tooth-pick. I never knew what they were, but I carefully picked them out to avoid eating them. The whole dish was covered with a top layer of cheese, sometimes toasted and partially burned, which made it crunchy and even better. Still one of my favorite meals.

Mom also made something called "Welsh rarebit," which I think was mainly cheese, but I didn't like it. I thought it sounded way too much like "rabbit."

Mr. Simmons, a friendly neighbor down the street, was a bodybuilder who had a son in the Air Force. He taught me how to do an extremely loud whistle using four fingers. I, in turn, taught the method to Royce, and when we whistled together, a strange harmonic note would often be produced that sounded very weird. It seemed to be more inside my head than outside.

Something that crept into popular use around this time was the custom of saying, "I don't know, but . . . " before making any statement of opinion. Maybe it had to do with the fact that there were so many rumors floating around all the time that it was hard to know what to believe. You would hear people say things like "I don't know, but I heard there isn't gonna be any more chewing gum soon. It's all going to the army." Or "I don't know, but you might not want to drop that Jap 20 millimeter cannon shell your brother sent you."

Speaking of things sent by male relatives overseas, there was a neat trick some of us were able to pull on friends who had never seen it before. You would get a little box and cut a hole in the bottom and line it with cotton, maybe dab a little Mercurochrome on the cotton, then stick your middle finger up through the hole. Then you would paint the finger yellow, get some dirt on it and use the Mercurochrome again make the base look bloody, bend the finger over and shut the lid of the box down on it. Then you would carry it to school with you and tell your friends conspiratorially, "Hey, you wanna see what my brother sent me from Tarawa? A dead Jap's finger!" And as they gathered around, you would stealthily open the box and show them the finger. You could even, after they had all been amazed, make the finger stand up and give them the finger! Keen!

But if you did it too much (and of course, you would), then word would get around and the goons would come for you. The idea was to ditch the box and hide the colorful hand in your pocket, but sometimes the concerned official would catch that. In my case, this led to another opportunity to discuss current events with the principal, Mr. McClain. I do believe he tried to hide a smile by turning his back and looking out the window that time.

Another phrase that was frequently heard among us was "Where do you get off?" It was used to express outrage or disbelief. I think this one may well have originated pre-war and perhaps have come from using the New York subway system.

Chapter 24

Sea Stories

A great many ships were crossing the Atlantic safely now, bringing supplies and men to England for the invasion. Our refugee friends, Miesje and her mother, Olive, had put their names on the list of people desiring passage back to England years before but never had been able to get space. A slot had finally opened up for them and they took it quickly. It was on a small troopship, and Miesje remembers it being very hot. Unfortunately, it was not a good time to go back to London.

The invasion came on June 6, and a week later, the V-1 flying bombs started falling around the London area. Some people have expressed the opinion that if the V-1 bombardment had started several months earlier and been as heavy as Hitler had wanted it to be, the invasion could not have been successfully mounted. But that idea completely overlooks the fact that the response would have been an overwhelming effort by all the airpower available, both British and American, to blanket the launch sites *and* their supply routes with a rain of explosives, day and night. It would have been very hard on the French civilians.

Miesje and her mother got back to England in July, just in time to experience this "second blitz," the bombardment by flying bombs, which in some ways was worse than the first blitz, because there was much less warning when a bomb was coming. Then, in September, it got even worse because of the V-2s: large rockets with a two-hundred-mile range and a one-ton warhead that crashed down from space with no warning at all. Since they arrived supersonically, the first noise anyone would hear was the crack of the sonic boom, followed instantly by the crash of the explosion. Living with this always hanging over their heads tended to make people a little jumpy.

There was an attempt to kill Hitler by blowing him up with a bomb in a conference room, hatched by just a few German officers, but many others were aware of it. It failed and many, many officers in the German Army and over a thousand civilian officials were tortured savagely and killed for it. Hitler survived, but in damaged condition, and seemed to make even worse decisions after that.

Various books will tell you that Hitler was insane and paranoid—that he thought everyone was trying to kill him. Well, there were at least eighty plots to kill him and they all failed. Psychopath, yeah . . . but paranoid? He wasn't wrong; a lot of people *were* trying to kill him.

In the Pacific we had learned from the bloody lesson of Tarawa, and now we blanketed a target island with incredible amounts of explosive shells and bombs. Sometimes it seemed that the Japanese defenders were just too dazed to mount a competent defense.

Our newest bombers, the very large B-29s, were having serious teething troubles (mainly involving engine fires), but nevertheless, they carried out their first raid on Japan from bases in China. Huge efforts were made to make the China-based B-29 raids work, but they were never very effective. What we needed were bases nearer to the targets and entirely under American control. The Marianas Islands in the Pacific, south of Japan, seemed to offer a likely solution, so we invaded the Marianas. This ignited a tremendous series of battles. One of the chief ones was at sea, a naval air battle now known as the Marianas Turkey Shoot. The famous name came about because our well-trained pilots, flying a superior airplane (the Grumman Hellcat), shot down almost four hundred badly trained Japs in one day, then sank some of their carriers the next, and someone remarked, "It was just like an old-time turkey shoot down home." We soon took the Marianas Islands and immediately started building a number of long runways for B-29s.

Many history books will tell you that biological warfare was never used during the war, but the Japanese did attempt it. A shipment of containers carrying plague-infected fleas was on its way to Saipan during the fighting but was sunk by one of our submarines on the way.

After the war, we found out that the Marine sergeant who told his men "C'mon, you guys, they can kill ya but they can't eat ya!" had also been wrong, for sometimes the starving enemy did eat parts of our dead troops.

That summer we went up to the farm in Connecticut again to see our cousins. On the property next to theirs, there were some young men who would put on a great fireworks show on the Fourth of July. They were building a big, long, V-shaped launching trough. We hung around watching them all afternoon and when nighttime finally came, we hugely enjoyed their show. They had some impressively large rockets that sailed grandly out over the valley before exploding. Great fun!

The Ringling Brothers, Barnum & Bailey circus came to Hartford, Connecticut, that year, and we all intended to go see it. But the night we were planning to attend, it was so hot that the family decided not to go. That night, during the performance, the big tent caught fire and, in the worst disaster in circus history, burned to the ground, killing 169 people and badly injuring 412. It was very fortunate that we stayed home.

I believe we went to Haversham on the Rhode Island coast again that year as well. I am not sure whether it was this year or in 1945 that we were visited by the blimp. Blimps had been found to be excellent weapons against U-boats, and there were more and more of them around. One of their main training bases was nearby.

It was a cold, clammy sort of day with a very thick fog when we heard a loud buzzing sound coming closer and closer, then going away, then coming back. It was up in the air! We all, grown-ups and kids, ran out of the house to see what it was. It came closer, right overhead, and out of the fog above us, a huge, gray balloon appeared, only about a hundred feet up. Then a man appeared in an open gondola window, and he was shouting a question at us. It seems they were lost. They knew they were over the coast somewhere, but couldn't figure out where.

"Which way is New London?" he was asking, and after a while, we understood him, so we all pointed to the west. He said, "Thank you," and they buzzed away. So that was our big memory for that summer. For a bunch of kids, it was tremendously exciting. It had never occurred to us that you could communicate with a blimp by just shouting back and forth. It probably would have been a lot harder had there been any wind.

In late October, we started to hear reports of another huge naval battle, this one in the waters around the Philippines. Our troops had landed on the island of Leyte, and General MacArthur had waded ashore, fulfilling his promise to return. The Japanese had reacted strongly to this threat by sending almost their entire navy to do battle with ours. The series of battles, called the "Battle for Leyte Gulf", lasted for days and was the biggest naval battle of all time. Toward the end, when Admiral Halsey, (whose nickname was "Bull Halsey" in some quarters) had been lured north with his entire fleet to chase after the Jap carriers (some referred to this as the "Battle of Bull's Run"), a very strong Japanese force emerged from between some of the islands and pounced on a small group of our little escort carriers. In a running battle, which by all rights should have seen the sinking of all six of our little carriers, only one was lost. The carrier group's escorts, only a few destroyers and even smaller destroyer escorts, put up an incredibly valiant and ferocious fight, and the enemy fleet attracted swarms of our aircraft, whose numbers increased steadily as the morning went on. In the end, three Japanese cruisers were sunk and their entire fleet turned around and headed back to Japan.

Maxie's Soda Shop was a little way up the street from our school, and when I was in the fifth grade, some of us used to wander up there during lunch hour. My main memory of that time is of seeing a newspaper at Maxie's that carried the headline: McCain's Fleet Racing Back to Battle. It sounded like he was the cavalry coming to save the settlers. Since reading that headline, I have always liked the name. That McCain was the grandfather of the present Senator John McCain.

Another thing I saw at that soda shop was a poster high up on the wall. It advertised Rhiengold Beer and showed the woman who was Miss Rhiengold that year. She was a redhead, and I thought she was exceptionally beautiful. It may have been the first time I ever reacted to what you might call a "pin-up." I don't know why Maxie would have had a poster of Miss Rhiengold in his shop; I'm pretty sure he couldn't sell beer. Maybe he, too, thought Miss Rhiengold was very pretty and just liked to look at her . . .

Her name was Lucille Ball.

That year at Halloween, I went with Mom to find a pumpkin. There was a big lot at the side of Valley road, north of town, that seemed to have hundreds of them. We got a good one and brought it home, and Mom went to work. We cut it open and scraped all the seeds out and made some eyes, but she didn't stop there. Mom didn't want her Jack-o'-lantern to be like all the others; she wanted it to have more character. She made ears out of green peppers cut in half and hollowed out and gave it a big, ugly, red pepper nose. I think she even made some eyebrows out of green pepper slivers, all held on with toothpicks. I thought it looked hideous. But I guess that's the whole point, isn't it? To make them look so horrible that they scare away the evil spirits.

And a new evil spirit was now stalking our fleet in the Pacific. At the end of The Battle for Leyte Gulf, the Japanese had revealed a new tactic called *kamikaze*, which they would use with horrifying success until the end of the war. During the battle, *kamikazes* sank one of our small carriers and damaged two others. It took some time before we adjusted to the fact that from now on, any aircraft coming toward our ships was a potential suicide bomber, and that we had to devise an effective defense.

In fact, no completely effective defense was ever found.

Early in November, Roosevelt won his fourth election and remained our president. I don't think anyone I knew was particularly surprised. We had loud arguments about it, as kids do, but we might as well have been arguing about Joe Louis vs. Two-Ton Tony Galento.

FDR was the president. He always had been.

Also in November, the first raids on Japan by B-29s based in the Marianas started. The Marianas bases were a big improvement over the bases in China, where all the fuel for the bombers had to be flown in from India over the Himalayas.

The Japanese cities were like piles of tinder just waiting to be ignited and the B-29s could carry bomb loads four times heavier than had been used against Germany.

The strategic bombing advocates were about to be given another opportunity to prove their theories.

CHAPTER 25

Land Stories

At home in America, the stock market had reached an all-time high. There was no unemployment; we heard it said that anyone who wanted a job had one.

By this time, I think we were feeling pretty confident about the war. Yet progress in Europe had slowed. An attempt in September to knife through Holland and cross the Rhine at a place called Arnhem had been a very bloody failure. The British airborne troops had taken the north end of the big bridge across the Rhine, but were unable to hold this "bridge too far" in the face of fierce German counter-attacks. One unfortunate result of this failed action was that the V-2 rocket launch sites in Holland, which would have been cut off from their supplies had the operation succeeded, were able to continue firing on London for many more months.

Out of the roughly ten thousand troops they put in, the British were able to bring out only about two thousand. The whole sorry business had mostly been Field Marshall Montgomery's pet idea, though Eisenhower had certainly approved it. After this debacle, Monty's reputation was somewhat tarnished.

The rest of the long front across France and Belgium seemed to fall back into a quieter mode. It was now obvious that the war would not be over in 1944, but when spring came, we were sure we'd be able to invade Germany and finish it.

Then Hitler dealt us a horrifying surprise. In the Ardennes, the same area through which they had launched their extremely effective end-run in 1940, the German Army had secretly and cleverly built up a hidden force of thirty divisions spearheaded by one thousand of their best tanks. They were opposed by only six U.S. divisions, sadly lacking in anti-tank weapons, and since it was considered a quiet sector, they were not experienced veterans, but were new to combat.

The attack was launched on December 16 and quickly punched a deep hole in our front line. Many of our green troops just ran for the rear, and many of those that stood and fought were overwhelmed. After a few days, any map of our front line showed a big indentation pointing toward Antwerp, which gave the "Battle of the Bulge" its name.

Our major problem was the weather. Allied aircraft were kept on the ground because of a thick fog that hung like a heavy blanket over everything. Under this blanket, free from harassment by our fighter-bombers, the Germans forged ahead.

The reaction at home (once the gravity of the event sunk in), was amazement and grim depression. We had thought that the Germans were on their last legs and just about ready to cave in. People had even started to think about what peacetime would be like and to make plans accordingly. It had been shocking to find that the German Army was still capable of mounting such an overwhelming attack, and this led to some overreaction on our end. We felt we had badly fooled ourselves into overconfidence.

Rationing, which had been quietly removed from many items, came back with a vengeance, and we were told that many items, such as shoes and tires, were going to be even scarcer. Now we were allowed only one pair of shoes per year instead of two. There was no rubber for rubber-soled shoes. I hated my leather-soled shoes; they slipped and slid when climbing or running, which could really be dangerous.

But then, around Christmas, the news started to improve. The weather over the battle in the Ardennes began to clear, and our fighter-bombers and supply planes were finally able to get up and start punishing the enemy. At that point, the Germans began to lose their momentum and to literally run out of gas. They had planned to at least partly fuel their drive with captured American gasoline, but had failed to do so. In the end, they had to destroy or abandon a great many tanks and other vehicles because they simply had no fuel. In another week or two, the Battle of the Bulge was just about over, though it did take almost another month before the Germans were beaten back to their starting line. They'd lost a hundred-thousand men and over eight hundred tanks, none of which could ever be replaced. We also lost heavily—81,000 American and 1,400 British soldiers—but according to General Eisenhower, we'd be able to replace our losses in a few weeks. That sounded pretty confident, but it also happened that many soldiers in the U.S. suddenly had their training stopped and were quickly hustled onto troopships bound for Europe.

1945

Chapter 26

Wind and Songs

On the last night of 1944, I think we again went down to the Wells' house to celebrate New Year's Eve. Once more, I was impressed by the great rising wail of sound that came up like a huge wind from all around the horizon at midnight. Sometimes I thought the sound was almost scary, as if the world herself were wailing. Not a wail of fear or sadness, either. Oh no, more like the angry, freaked-out *warning* cry of a gigantic, cornered cat—a cat that didn't like what the little parasites on her skin were doing. They were making her itch.

I was thinking of the war, not ecology. Nobody was very concerned about ecology then. I think the general reasoning was "Let's win the war first, then we can worry about the fumes." And the beaches covered with oil . . .

We had another cold winter that year. I saw the mercury in Grandpa's old thermometer on the front porch drop below zero several times. Huffing your breath out hard made a lot of vapor, and when you drew a long sniff in through your nose, you could feel the hairs in it freeze up. Sometimes, as you walked on snowy streets, especially on a night with no wind, the snow would crunch and squeak with every step.

Mom taught me that if the leaves of the rhododendron bushes curled up (tightly, lengthwise) it meant the temperature was below freezing.

At school I was in the fifth grade, and a number of new kids had showed up. They had been going to other elementary schools nearby but were now combined into classes in our larger, central school. Fifth grade was split into two sections, in separate but adjacent rooms. Mrs. Smith and Mrs. McCoy, who taught the two sections, were good enough friends that every year they went on vacation together to Mexico, which seemed to be a place they really liked.

I don't know if concentrating on Mexico was a normal part of the school curriculum for fifth grade, or if it was because our two teachers were so hipped on it, but we sure did hear a lot about Mexico that year. We even sang songs about it:

"A Mexican trip is pleasant. We'll speak to a brown-eyed peasant . . . "

Oh, brother . . . Some things will stick with you forever.

We also learned a lot of Stephen Foster songs, and they will stick with you, too.

A lot of them are kinda sad, you know? "Old dog Tray . . . grief cannot drive him away . . . " (Why grief? What's he sad about? Whatsamatta?) "All the world is sad and dreary," "Weep no more, my lady," "Bye 'n' bye, hard times come a-knockin' at the door . . . " Never understood that line in fifth grade. I imagined ole "Hard Times" to be a sort of scruffy, dirty old bum with a cigar stub in his mug, sort of like the famous circus clown Emmett Kelly. I do seem to remember one or two unfamiliar men, strangers who knocked on our back door way back in 1937 or '38, I guess. But they didn't look like Emmett Kelly; they just looked like tough, tired men who were a little dirty. Those were still depression years.

But later in life . . . well, sooner or later, we all get a little taste of what that line about "hard times" really means.

And hearing your lady weep can be like a knife in your heart.

Fortunately, kids don't know about that stuff yet. Instead of singing, I think many of us just mouthed the words and made some noises while thinking about baseball scores and airplanes and maybe pudgy Miss Mooney's circular pitch pipe.

I did like to sing "Take my duds an tote 'em on my back when the Glendy Burk comes down." That sounded like fun to me. The guy was movin' on. I liked the idea of the "Camptown ladies singin' that song, Doo-Dah, Doo-Dah," too.

A song called "Mairzy Doats," which had actually come out in 1943, beat all records for sales of sheet music and became the freak hit of the decade. It had some double-talk in it and didn't make much sense, but everybody sang it anyhow.

I think the song "One Meat Ball" may have gotten big around this time (we thought it was new, but it had actually originated in the 1850s). The chorus went, "You get no bread with one meat ball," which we enjoyed saying to each other for a while. We thought it was funny. Japanese airplanes were called "meatballs" then because of the insignia on their wings, which were red circles.

Another song that became popular was "Chickery Chick, Cha-la Cha-la." This was another sort of double-talk song. It bothered and irritated me that I didn't know the words to it and didn't know how to find them. I felt out of it. I would hear bits of it being sung by people, usually older girls, and I would try to catch the rest but I never could. (Now I think that may have been because they didn't know them either.) I had mastered all the words to "Mairzy Doats" without trouble while other people had found them mysterious. But that song was easy to pick up; it had been played constantly on the radio. Magazine articles had even been written about it, providing all the words. Bing Crosby even sang it on *Your Hit Parade*.

But "Chickery Chick, Cha-la Cha-la" was not so easy. I imagine that very few people knew that it dated back to the 1770s or that it had originally concerned a complicated Chinese name. I certainly didn't, and the words *still* remain a mystery to me. After "chickery-chick, cha-la cha-la" the next words the girls seemed to sing sounded something like "Sackalaroamy, in a banannico" but that's about all the more hep I ever got.

Yeah, hep. "Hip" wasn't hep yet.

"Don't Fence Me In" was another song that came out then. That's a song I've always liked. That may have been near the beginning of a great wave of enthusiasm for cowboys and the American west that swept through popular music and movies and has lasted for many, many years.

The bombing campaign against the Japanese homeland was still not showing the results we'd hoped for. Since the beginning of the war, the great hope of the Air Force leaders had been that a bomber could be developed that was big enough and had enough range to reach the Japanese homeland and introduce them to the benefits of strategic bombing.

The B-29 Superfortress had looked like it was going to be the airplane to do the job, but the urgency to get it into action had caused the program to be too rushed. The plane's many mechanical problems had been largely overcome by now, but a new problem was beginning to show itself.

The Superfort was pressurized and designed to fly so high that most fighters and anti-aircraft shells of the time couldn't even reach it. But at that altitude, for the first time, they began to experience something unknown and mysterious, but which we now hear about daily: the jet stream. The stream was blowing strongly over Japan that winter and the effect it had on accurate bombing often led to ludicrous results. Flying into the wind, the aircraft's ground speed could sometimes fall so low that it seemed to be barely moving, and going downwind, its speed could climb to unheard-of levels. The effects of crosswind were even worse. We were not told much about it, but I well remember hearing on the radio "Our bombers are approaching Japan at 440 miles per hour!" and feeling smugly impressed that we had developed such a marvelously speedy bomber. At the time, our Flying Fortresses in Europe were commonly approaching their targets at speeds around 160 mph.

In January a new general went out to the Pacific to take over the B-29 effort against Japan. His name was Curtis LeMay.

Curt LeMay has become a somewhat controversial historical figure, but whatever else may be true about him, he was a consummate, unemotional, no-nonsense professional, given a job to do by his country that he did very well. Decisions he made undoubtedly shortened the war by many months and saved many American lives—no telling how many.

For several months he tried to follow the Air Force's traditional strategy of precision bombing, but it wasn't that his predecessor hadn't been trying hard enough; the mistake lay in trying to fight Aeolus and Maria. The gods and goddesses of wind always won.

There were kamikazes at 30,000 feet, too. Some Jap planes were able to get up to the B-29s' altitude and wait for them (most of the enemy aircraft would have had a very hard time trying to catch up from behind). Then they would attack us head-on, ending in an attempt to collide with us at a combined speed of 500 to 600 miles per hour. Some of them were successful.

The small volcanic island of Iwo Jima was located about halfway between the B-29 bases in the Marianas and Japan. Japanese aircraft based there became a problem. They could intercept our bombers heading for Japan and hit them again on their way back. They also made some surprise, one-way trips to our Marianas bases that were startlingly successful. In at least one of these raids, we lost three of our bombers, burned up and exploded on the ground. There was even one instance when a Japanese pilot, exhibiting an incredible amount of . . . something, used up all his ammunition strafing, then *landed* his airplane and *got out*, firing his pistol. Many American ground crew and soldiers were delighted to have the chance to blaze away at him and give him what he wanted.

Can't you just see the commanding general hopping up and down in a frenzy, screaming, "Don't hit our bombers! Careful! Don't hit the bombers!"?

Iwo Jima would make a very good emergency field for our damaged bombers to land at, too, so it became our next island target.

I think the story of the battle for Iwo Jima is pretty well known, no need to rehash it, but for weeks at home it seemed to be the only thing people talked about. Day after day, there were new headlines, newspaper stories, and radio coverage. At the movies, there were news clips and eventually special news shorts just about the battle. It went on for over a month.

There was a growing sense of horror in America; the war seemed to be escalating in carnage by huge leaps with every island we invaded. The Japs' basic idea by this time was that if they made each step closer to their homeland more costly for us, sooner or later we would search for a way to end the fighting without having to invade Japan.

There were some Americans, many of them mothers, who agreed.

CHAPTER 27

My Medal

One of the biggest things in my life that spring was the "General Eisenhower Waste Paper Collection Campaign." We learned about it in Cub Scouts. The deal was, if you collected one thousand pounds of paper and you turned it in, you would get a medal for it. A *real* medal! That was a big deal for some of us, that medal. Kind of like a Captain Midnight decoder badge, but better. This wasn't some cloth badge that Mom sewed on your Cub Scout shirt for you; this was a *real medal!*

I don't know why paper had suddenly become scarce; it may be that a lot of trees were being used for other things. Plywood was certainly being used in a lot of wartime products (like landing craft). The housewives of America were being urged to use their paper grocery bags over and over again, and I several times helped Mom by flattening those big bags out.

The American (and British) public had become a little gun-shy about scrap drives by this time. Aunt Ernestine had turned in her best girdle and now regretted it, and many a housewife now wished she hadn't given up her good old aluminum cooking pot.

The aluminum drive was especially resented when the rumor made the rounds that they couldn't just melt down old aluminum pots and pans and make P-38s out of them anyhow. Aircraft aluminum is a much better, tougher alloy. So the people who ran the scrap drive now had mountains of old pots and pans, and they didn't know what to do with them. Finally, the story went, they'd ground up all those pots and pans into powder and mixed it with other stuff to make flares and star-shells.

Unfortunately, that was one of those rumors that turned out to be true.

But evidently the paper really was needed, and the drive went ahead. So I went to work collecting paper, mostly newspapers. I dragged my wagon all over the neighborhood. I knocked on many doors and lined up all the friendly neighbors. Seems to me it was only newspaper the general was interested in. I got my pile up to a thousand pounds in a month or so. One or the other parent must have driven me and my half-ton of paper to the church basement where they weighed it. I'm sure I didn't carry it all downtown by myself.

So I got my medal. I still have it, too. You don't think I would throw away my *medal*, do you?

Some years ago, for a reunion, I got it out of my box of memorabilia. (Jenny calls it "junk" but she just doesn't appreciate the true value of antiquities.) It looked pretty sad, but I fixed it all up. I painted the diagonal stripes bright red and white, and I painted the medal itself bright gold (gold paint is a lot better now than it was in 1945.) I have it mounted in a small, bright gold frame on a bright blue background with the inscription mounted beneath, "Awarded for Extraordinary Patriotic Achievement," just like it says on the medal. You know, the same way some people display their real medals in dens and home offices.

To date, nobody has ever bothered to look at my medal closely enough to get the joke.

Mom was driving up Bradford Avenue on her way back from shopping one day and she saw a very strange thing coming down the hill at her: a baby carriage with a small, chunky, redheaded kid in it. It was one of her former Cub Scouts, Charlie Martin.

Charlie had also been collecting newspapers to get his medal. He was using a baby carriage to carry them in. He had been poaching on *my* territory!

Mom was usually the complete opposite of what you'd call a "busybody" (and she actively discouraged it in others), but this was too much for her. She saw one of her former Cub Scouts engaging in what must have surely looked like life-threatening behavior, and she couldn't stand it!

I think—I *know*—that she thought of us all as "her kids," then and later. So she stopped and read Charlie the Riot Act. He, being well trained to be polite to his elders, probably saluted obediently and resumed his small thrill-ride as soon as he safely could.

This is a story that Mom loved to tell to people later on. Whenever I overheard it, the same thoughts would run through my mind:

One: "That must have been a really *neat* thing to do! I wish *I'd* done that!"

And Two: "He was poaching in *my* territory!"

On the night of February 13, almost eight hundred British bombers went to Dresden, and Bomber Harris finally got another firestorm. This one was even bigger than Hamburg, at least in terms of mortality. Dresden had been filled with German refugees, most of whom were fleeing the advancing Russians (who were not known for their forgiving attitudes towards Germans). The USAAF went in with a 450-plane raid the next day, and after that Dresden was no longer on the target list.

The German defenses were very weak by this time, so our losses were miniscule. Most histories put the figure for total immediate deaths somewhere above 130,000 (mostly civilians and far more than in either Hiroshima or Nagasaki.)

But the 13th turned out to be bad luck for everyone involved. Many people, both here and in England, thought that it was too much, that it smacked of the needless murder of women and children (which it surely was) at a time when the enemy was obviously beaten. The storm of disapproval grew until Churchill, who had originally approved the policy that Harris had been following, started trying to distance himself from it, both then and in his memoirs.

Like LeMay years later, for Harris it was the sad story of a professional, capable, single-minded and extremely stubborn warrior's reputation suffering because he did his assigned job too thoroughly and became a convenient political scapegoat.

Some thought that the attack might have been carried out in part to impress the fast-approaching Russians, to awe them with the huge strength of their allies' air forces, our ability to erase a big city with a single raid.

The Russians just shrugged. Erased cities were nothing new to them.

We heard plenty about this one, both by radio and newspaper. But I don't remember hearing anyone cluck-clucking about the huge death toll, and I don't remember hearing my parents saying much about it. They may have talked about it in the kitchen, behind a closed door. (I realize now that that's where they went to get away from "little pitchers," i.e., children, while dealing with the dishes.)

I think that by this time, grown-ups may have become careful about what they said around their children. It was never as bad as it was among the Nazis, where, what with fascism and the Hitler Youth program, kids found themselves in possession of leverage that most kids could only dream of. A German kid who had been disciplined a few times by beating (which was then the universally accepted method of bringing understanding to children, both there and here,) could go to the Gestapo and tell them that his father had called Hitler a Jew. That might get rid of dear old Dad quite easily. If not, it would certainly make him a lot more careful—and more polite to young Klaus in the future.

But kids do talk and sometimes misinterpret what they hear, and then it gets back to some other kid's parent, who may or may not have some sort of unknown agenda. I do remember hearing lowered voices behind the kitchen door and that line "Little pitchers have big ears" a few times.

I don't know, but I suspect that my mother, with her love of antiques and appreciation of beauty, and that my father, with his love of ancient architecture, probably deplored the raid. The two of them, before the war, had a tradition of going into New York City on Labor Day, where they would stroll up and down the avenues, looking at and appreciating the designs of the buildings. They certainly weren't "Puttin' on the Ritz," though, and my father didn't look much like Gary Cooper (but later on, I did think that he and Jimmy Stewart began to look disturbingly a lot alike).

Why Labor Days? Nobody home. The city would be more or less deserted. Everybody had gone to the beach.

There was almost no fear of being mugged in daylight then. I say again: we've lost a lot.

Among my friends in the fifth grade, any talk about Dresden would have gone something like:

"What the Hell? They were Germans, weren't they?"

"But a lot of them were women and children."

"So what? They started it, didn't they? They just got what they deserved!"

Sounds kinda heartless now, doesn't it?

"You don't like it, you know what you kin do!"

I already told you, things were different then. That's just the way it was.

CHAPTER 28

The War Comes Closer

In Europe, the Battle of the Bulge was over and the Germans were pushed back to about where they had started, but they still fought skillfully for every foot, especially on German soil. Getting across the Rhine looked like it was going to take a full-blown amphibious landing—much like the Normandy invasion—plus a full-scale airborne drop of as many paratroopers as we could lift. It promised to be a very bloody affair.

Hitler had ordered that every bridge across the Rhine be blown up, and had threatened immediate death for the commander responsible if there was any failure.

But then, all at once, word was that our troops had found an intact bridge over the Rhine at Remagen, Germany. We stormed across the bridge, the responsible German commander was shot, and we had a foothold in Germany. Suddenly that was what everyone was talking about.

That and the kamikazes. The kamikazes just reinforced what everyone already thought:

"The Japs are not sane and they're not human. They are just a bunch of crazy animals, and the only possible approach we can take is to treat them like mad dogs: kill them all, or kill so many of them that they finally quit, and then put some kind of fence around the rest of 'em!"

Yet from that time until the war's end, those kamikazes ("Divine Wind" in Japanese) sank and damaged enough ships of the U.S. Navy to seriously frighten navy leaders, whose challenge lay in finding a defense that worked. I imagine knocking down a kamikaze was sort of like trying to shoot a small duck that's diving out of the sun, going as fast as he can, straight *at* you or the duck blind next to you.

The Japanese also started using kamikaze motorboats and manned torpedoes to attack our ships. Finally, they hit upon the most amazing thing of all: the *Okha*. It looked kind of like a short torpedo with wings and a tail, rocket-propelled and barely controlled (at 600 mph) by a barely-trained pilot. These missiles were soon called not *Okha*, but "Baka Bombs" by our men. *Baka* means something like "nutty-stupid" in Japanese. Most of them went into the water, one way or another, but they did nail a few of our ships.

At Iwo Jima, our flag had been raised on Mt. Suribachi. A photo of the flag raising was eventually published all around the world and became perhaps the most famous picture to come out of the war.

At the time I was unimpressed. I thought the flag should have been standing straight out. Yes, I know. Remember, I was ten.

At home, it seemed the pace of events had somehow picked up. Things seemed to be happening one right after the other, in rapid succession.

Rationing came back, hard. It didn't affect me, but cigarettes just about disappeared. My father smoked Chesterfields, sometimes Camels. I always liked to look at the scenes on the packs—Egypt, I suppose, or someplace like that. I don't remember him being unable to get cigarettes, but I have read that some stores would only allow one carton per customer, and then only known, loyal customers. It wasn't rationing; cigarettes just didn't exist. I have no idea why; maybe there was a bad crop. The winter of '45 had been a very bad one. But there were plenty of cigs for servicemen. Maybe they got them all.

Butter disappeared, too. So did many brands of soap. I wouldn't know why. But margarine got a big boost in popularity that it has never lost. Didn't even have to knead that little drop of blood into it any more.

A dire warning was issued for the east coasts of the U.S. and Canada about robotic flying bombs. It was not just *possible* that we would be hit by them—it was probable! What made the announcement even more interesting was that it also said that this warning was similar to the one issued on the last election day, a few months prior in 1944, which no one remembered hearing.

Evidently there had been a huge flap, and a large number of our airplanes had been sent to Long Island to stage out of there to search the Atlantic for missile-launching U-boats. It seems that one missile had been detected (no doubt a V-1—we launched a few captured ones ourselves from our own subs after the war) and had then disappeared. It almost certainly just flew into the water. I've taken this story from what Andy Rooney, who witnessed them, wrote about the events.

In the late '40s, using a concept very much like the V-1, the Northrup Corporation began designing a much bigger, faster, higher-flying, *far* more complicated and *much* less reliable intercontinental guided missile that was theoretically capable of carrying a thermonuclear warhead to a target nearly 7,000 miles away. But it was pretty much the same idea as an overgrown V-1: they both had wings and were propelled by a single jet engine.

This later missile was called the "Snark." The word seems to have a different meaning now, but in 1960, a Snark was a long, gray cruise missile, actually even a little longer than a Flying Fortress. As an ex-Snark launch officer, I can tell you categorically that it, like the V-1, seemed to like water and would frequently go for a swim whenever it was sent down-range from Canaveral. (Or it might, without asking permission, suddenly take a right and go visit Brazil instead . . . twice.)

Rooney said that he never did get a straight answer from the military about whether or not an incoming missile had ever been spotted or attacked and that he'd still like to know. I would too, but unless I hear it from some pretty mature army pilot or member of a long-gone U-boat crew, I doubt I ever will. This story, like hundreds of other undoubtedly fascinating WWII stories, will simply disappear—like Amelia whatshername.

In the Pacific, General LeMay had been experimenting with various bombing methods and the one that seemed to work the best was to bring the bombers down to a much lower altitude, load them up with as many incendiaries as they could possibly carry, and send them over Japan at night, just like the British had been doing to the Germans, and the Germans to the British before that. Starting in 1915, as a matter of fact.

On March 9, the B-29s made a very big raid on Tokyo that burned out ten square miles of the city. That's a lot.

Then we invaded Okinawa on April Fool's Day. Before that battle was over, many would reflect on the date and wonder if it hadn't been a huge, cruel joke on us after all; but in the beginning, by and large, the Marines just walked ashore without much trouble. Maybe, after our immense pre-landing bombardment of the beaches, it did seem to be some a sort of joke, but things got a lot rougher later on.

CHAPTER 29

Historic Figures Leave the Stage

Things were happening fast now, but time seemed to come to a halt and stand still on April 12, when we heard of the president's death. It was late afternoon, and I can still see the corner of the sunlit wall in our house I was staring at, wondering how things would change. It was sort of like hearing that a grandfather who lived in another city had died: sad, but bearable, somewhat removed from my real life.

But kids my age had never known a different president. He had just seemed to always be there, like a big, benevolent father figure who was omnipresent, maybe a bit like Uncle Sam. Subsequent changes in leadership wouldn't affect my generation the same way. When Franklin Delano Roosevelt died, there was the feeling that we should somehow be shattered with grief, but strangely were not. Maybe "numb" is the best word to describe how we felt, or "bewildered," wondering what would come next.

FDR had operated with a rather imperial manner, which I have always thought fitting for the leader of the most powerful nation on earth. I have never been able to shake the feeling that every president since him has been an impostor.

And yet, as far as losses go, it was surprisingly easy to get over. I didn't notice any adults collapsing in sorrow, either. I think they were mostly curious and wondering what the new president would be like.

Soon enough we found out that it was going to be business as usual.

One weekend while I was outside in our yard, the world filled with the roaring sounds of single-engine airplanes, following one after the other, low and fast toward the slope of the First Watchung. They were making simulated torpedo drops, then peeling up and away to the left and right, directly over my head. They were Grumman Avengers, Navy Torpedo planes that had been getting a lot of press coverage lately for their work in the Pacific. They appeared to be using the long ridge of the mountain as a surrogate for a Jap ship, and their runs seemed to me to be made with a *lot* of energy and zest, like maybe they were showing off. I have often wondered since what the occasion might have been, and I have fantasized that they knew very well that they would be disciplined and didn't care, for they were about to ship out to the Pacific. By then, everyone who got orders for the Pacific knew that an invasion of Japan was coming next, that it would be a God-awful, hideous bloodbath, and that a lot of them would probably not be coming back. The air show went on for about fifteen minutes and then was suddenly over.

Who knows? Maybe it was just done to impress someone's girlfriend or parents.

We also saw a lot of DC-3s and DC-4s flying around all the time. We were right under the flyway into Newark, and there were always Eastern Airlines DC-3s passing overhead. There were also frequent Army DC-3s, painted olive drab (they were officially called "Skytrains," and the British called them "Dakotas", but they have ever since been called "Gooney Birds" by everyone else). They all made the same noise: "Dirdle-dirdle-dirdle dirdlum dirdlum dirdlum lum lum lummm . . . " It was a nice, relaxed, soothing sort of sound. Now, the sound of an airliner climbing out over the same area is like hearing an avalanche coming . . . also enjoyable, but not exactly soothing.

There were occasional B-17s, too. Nowadays you might see one trundling by at an airshow. In the company of a newer, larger aircraft, they can seem almost small. But in those days, the Flying Fortress was considered to be a heavy bomber and had won great fame in battles over Europe. It was exciting as hell to see and hear one fly over. That sound was unique, and I still can recognize it all these years later.

I can't say whether this memory is from the late war years or immediately after the war's end, but for several years there was a five-engined B-17 that flew over our house frequently. It had the normal four engines on the wings and another big one in the nose where the bombardier would normally sit. It had a unique sound, and I well remember once seeing it flying over using only the engine in the nose. I've since learned that I was seeing a flying testbed for the engine that would eventually go on the huge six-engine B-36 (another airplane with a sound that, once heard, can never be forgotten).

I don't remember seeing many other kinds of aircraft in the sky during those days, and I think I would have noticed had they been there. (By now I think it's possible you've noticed a certain interest in aircraft on my part).

There were occasional Navy Hellcats (F6Fs) but what I longed for and never did see was a P-38. That Lockheed twin-boomed fighter had been my favorite for a long time. Because of its long range, it had been an obvious choice for assignment to the Pacific theater. Several famous pilots out there had set what were, for American pilots, all-time high scores of enemy aircraft downed while flying it. Even Charles Lindbergh, flying as a "civilian advisor," had shot down a Jap while flying one.

Our troops had overrun Germany now, and the Russians had done the same from the other side. The battle for Berlin was intense, vicious, and unrelenting, and the Russians showed no mercy toward the people who had savagely and brutally invaded their homeland four years earlier.

Then, before the Russians could get to him and make an exhibition of him, Hitler killed himself in his bunker, and suddenly the war in Europe was over. V-E day was declared on May 8. The Europeans went wild with joy and many Americans tried to, too, but we had unfinished business in the Pacific and knew very well that it was going to be horrendous. The celebrating was tempered by a latent sense of foreboding.

And all this time, in the Pacific, the kamikazes kept on coming, sinking our ships. The British had sent some ships out there to join us around Okinawa, and the kamikazes mostly just bounced off them without doing much damage. The British carriers had armored flight decks, and I suspect many American admirals wished they did, too.

CHAPTER 30

A Different Quarry

B ack home, Royce and I were planning our second camping adventure. During the previous year, we had taken a hike together to camp out overnight, but had only gotten as far as a place near the reservoir. The only really interesting thing to happen on that trip was that we saw a very *big* brown dog running around in the woods quite a distance from us. Royce had been pretty sure it was a bear, and I was half convinced, but it didn't pay any attention to us. We decided that on our next trip, we would penetrate the unknown areas beyond those we'd previously explored.

Spring had come, and one sunny weekend day, we started hiking north along the ridge of the First Watchung. We went far past the place where we had camped the year before, climbed down to a place where a road went through a shallow gap toward the reservoir, up the other side, and onward to the north. We were now in totally unfamiliar territory. We finally came to a place where the rocks led down to a big gap, and there was route 46, with cars roaring along it. You would think I would remember something as chancy as running across four lanes of busy highway with a dividing barrier in the middle, but I don't. We must have done it, though. (No doubt there were far fewer cars on the road then.) We went on up the other side and into rocks and woods, which are probably no longer there. I don't remember anything about the rest of our hike until we came to the end, which did indeed print an indelible scene on my mind.

We came to the edge of a deep quarry, one much wider and a little deeper than the one behind my house. A hundred feet below us, its floor was flat and bare, without any grass or trees, and seemed to be several hundred feet wide. A long, high, curving wall of rock had been left in place on the eastern side, which we naturally decided to walk out on. The wall of rock was amazing: it was only about three feet wide at the top, and out near the end, it fell vertically for at least a hundred feet on all sides, though it seemed like much more. It felt like we were ants balanced on top of a huge fence. We went out to the end and sat there in the sunlight, drinking in the vast scene before us. To the east, far beneath our feet were houses and trees that spread out into the distance, where they merged in the haze all the way to the edge of the world, to the line of shadowy-blue city buildings on the horizon. A little farther around to the south was another cluster of blue-gray buildings in Newark. The sun blazed down, everything seemed to shine brightly in the clear air, and the sky was dotted with small, white clouds. It was one of those moments you don't forget.

Recently I saw a TV program that described the geology of the land around the Hudson Palisades. It showed some big fossilized dinosaur footprints, discovered in a place called Clifton Quarry. There, in the cliff wall, hung a short line of footprints, walking across the rock, right at eye-level for the viewer. And that's right where we had been, looking down into a big quarry just west of Clifton. (Clifton! Cliff-town! How about that?)

Little did we know. It's probably just as well that we didn't see any dinosaur footprints, though. If we had, I'm sure I would have gone back later to try to pry one out of the wall somehow, and that might well have led to all *sorts* of problems.

From late August to October of that year, a big conference was being held in D.C. called the Dumbarton Oaks Conference. Dumbarton Oaks was a large estate near where my father had grown up in Georgetown, so he was very interested. I thought the name was kind of weird and would often say things like "That's pretty dumb, Barton." Which was only funny once and not very funny then.

That conference was the beginning of what became the United Nations.

Fighting was still going on in the Philippines. It seemed to go on forever, as did the battle of Okinawa. We put more resources into Okinawa than we did into the invasion of Normandy.

Huge fire raids on Japanese cities seemed to be announced almost daily. By this time, half of Tokyo, thirty-five square miles, was gone, and 4.5 million people were homeless. But still they fought on.

Terrible things were being discovered in Germany: concentration camps where millions of people had been deliberately killed. At first the stories were unbelievable, but more and more details were released and then the horrible photos . . .

I don't think we kids talked about it much. We would tell stories to each other of the awful things we had learned, but then we'd fall silent and just shake our heads.

"How can people *do* things like that?" the adults would say.

But knowing of the gas chambers and of the things being done in the Pacific, where any concept of "civilized warfare" had gone out the window long ago, and hearing tales of our troops and allies behaving just as badly at times in retaliation, I began to believe that all humans, *any* human, will commit unspeakable, hideous acts if pushed into a sufficiently dark, evil corner.

Ultimately, I think we kids didn't know *what* to say about it all, so we would just shake our heads and move on to more pertinent subjects, like how to blow a bigger bubble with our Bazooka bubblegum.

Royce was developing the ability to make a low whistle by cupping his hands together and blowing through the space between his two thumbs. He practiced this endlessly, trying to perfect it, and eventually got very good at it. It sounded like mourning doves calling. I was irritated because I couldn't seem to get the hang of it myself. Now, whenever I hear a mourning dove calling somewhere in the woods, I am reminded of my friend.

We also developed a fascination with lassos. We got some clothesline and started lassoing everything in sight. Of course, we lassoed my younger brother from time to time and graduated from that to other people's younger brothers.

I missed the great moment myself, not being around at the time, but Royce had evidently lassoed someone in his neighborhood, and the concerned father had sat him down and delivered a long, passionate lecture on the dangers of lassoing people that ended, with overdone sound effects and graphic dramatics, in a demonstration of what a human hanging looked like. Royce was impressed, more by the ridiculousness of the overacting than by anything else. But in any case, I think we soon got tired of lassos.

Fast-drying airplane glue suddenly became available again, and balsa wood came back, too (probably from a stockpile the government had been hoarding). I made models of many different airplanes, mostly fighters. It was a real joy to be able to quickly sand down a balsa-wood wing or tail. For some reason, the model I remember best was my P-47 Thunderbolt. The later versions of the '47 had grown a little longer and had bubble canopies; they didn't look so stubby as the faded brown gaggle I'd seen flying above the cliff only a few years (but a whole war) ago. I thought my silver model with a low-slung belly looked sleek and businesslike. I can still see it.

In the fifth grade we were still immersed in Mexican history and culture.

We were going to put on a big play about the Aztecs. We all got to wear strange-looking costumes, and Walt Davis, who was still (and would forever be) the tallest kid in the class, was the great god Quetzalcoatl. I think he even got to wear a big feathery headdress. I have called him Quetzalcoatl ever since.

There was a kid named McKelvey in the other fifth-grade section. I didn't know him well, but we were friendly. He seemed to have a good sense of humor. We all called him Mac. The last day of school finally came (a half day), and though it started out fairly normal, a sense of release and anticipation for the coming vacation fun started to build over the course of the day. Around noon, Mrs. McCoy left the room, and her class, the other fifth-grade section, inevitably began to come unglued. Of course the "good" kids (the girls and many of the boys), only looked on with horrified fascination, but some of the more adventuresome guys started to throw things out the windows. First it was just chalk, erasers, and maybe some books, but things rapidly escalated. I don't know why I was able to witness this, for I didn't belong in that classroom. I was out in the hall and just naturally gravitated toward the sound of rioting. I saw several small items go out the window and then I watched, amazed, as Mac picked up somebody's desk and emptied the *whole thing* out the window!

Mrs. McCoy soon reappeared. I don't know if she had witnessed Mac's great act of anarchy, or if someone tattled on him, but printed forever in my mind is the image of Mrs. McCoy shouting, "McKelvey, come back here!" and of Mac, taking off down the hall, his ears sticking out, leaning into the turn as he cornered, leaving behind only his defiant, echoing, "HAR HAR HAR!" as he disappeared, forever done with 5th grade.

"Now, there is one gutsy, free spirit!" I thought, "I want to get to know this guy better!"

Well, I certainly did, and our wonderful friendship spanned two centuries.

Then it was summer, and all the various things kids can do during summer took over. Of course, there was the quarry—a standing attraction for my friends. They would frequently wander up to my house, and we would climb all over the rocks and perch on the cliffs, looking out at the great sweep of land extending to the hazy horizon. It was a great place to just sit and be lazy. Some of my friends became very clever at persuading Mom to make lemonade and maybe produce some cookies, too.

We also haunted several other parks in town. There were boulders as big as cars in some of them—boulders that didn't belong there, left by melting glaciers 15,000 years before. I would look at them and think that probably they had the invisible paw prints of long-vanished saber-toothed cats on them.

My family and I went up to Rhode Island again. Everything was the same as it had been the year before, until one morning when we heard and saw a line of navy fighters, high in the sky, taking turns peeling off and diving down to pull out just above the beach. It looked as if they might be strafing something—maybe even a beached U-boat! This show continued for quite a while, so we all piled into the motorboat and went across the inlet to see what was going on. There was a Jeep with a long whip antenna parked there and a man standing beside it. When we got closer, we could see that there was a big, white cloth cross laid out on the sand. The airplanes, which were F6F Hellcats, were making practice diving runs on the cross, and the man, who was being called "Charlie" on the radio, was watching them through a hand-held device that looked like a bent flashlight. With it, you could sight a diving Hellcat and gauge the angle of its dive, which was what the pilots were practicing. "Charlie" told us that they were practicing rocket-firing runs. After each run, he would tell them on the radio how they had done. The airplanes would start their diving runs from about 5000 feet and seemed to come almost straight down at us, pulling out right over our heads at very low altitudes. Some of them couldn't have been any higher than fifty feet above us. I could clearly see rivets and oil streaks on some of them, and as they pulled out, the howl and thunder of noise was terrific. It was immensely exciting, one of the best air shows I've ever seen.

After that, the rest of the visit was boring, for Charlie and the Hellcats never came back, though every day we eagerly watched and hoped that they would.

CHAPTER 31

A Monster is Born

The war dragged on. Most of the interesting news from the Pacific was about the battle of Okinawa and the fire-bombing of Japan. It seemed that there was at least one big raid on Japan every two days, sometimes every day. Total bomb tonnages were now up around 3,500 tons per raid. Japan was swiftly being turned into a wasteland.

In the U.S., things called "Babushkas" had appeared earlier on women's heads as a new style of head covering, but they were really to prevent long hair from getting caught in war-plant machinery (several women had been virtually scalped). They now morphed into something called the "snood," which looked a little like a tight, sculpted turban, and I actually thought they looked pretty good—kind of sophisticated and classy. That's an idea I must have gotten from *Life* magazine.

The new phrase on everyone's lips was "Hubba, Hubba!" It could mean anything that was good or desirable. I heard it applied mostly to shapely women, but it could also mean anything else that was surprising or exciting. Evidently navy pilots also shouted it loudly as they raced for their planes on the flight decks.

By now we were sure we were going to win, and war news seemed almost boring.

Early one morning in July the dark sky above the New Mexican desert was ripped open from end to end by an immense light. Almost a minute later the nuclear scientists watching from ten miles away heard the long, drawn-out rumble as the monster they had created and loosed upon mankind awakened and cleared its throat. The newspapers were told only that a big ammunition dump had exploded, but the men of the Manhattan Project were both horrified and awe-struck by their success (and thankful that the earth itself had not caught fire).

In New Jersey, we heard nothing about it. There may have been a short article in the paper, but in those days, I didn't read newspapers. They seemed too grown-up and boring to me, nothing like the exciting pictures in *Life* magazine.

On June 22, it was announced that the battle of Okinawa was finally over. It had cost the Japanese 110,000 dead and about 7,400 prisoners (big change there—in the past almost none of them would have surrendered). It had cost us 7,000 dead with 29,000 wounded. We had also lost thirty-six ships, with 368 badly damaged, and the kamikazes were still coming down from Japan and crashing into our ships. They were starving, but they just wouldn't give up.

Anyone could see that if there wasn't a surrender (which seemed completely unlikely), an invasion of the enemy homeland would be sure to unleash such terrible carnage that it would make our casualties in Okinawa look small. It was bound to be a hideous wound on our entire population that would last for many generations into the future. No wonder Truman decided to use the atomic bomb.

On June 30, the Philippine campaign was declared over, but it really wasn't, since pockets of die-hard Japanese soldiers held out in the hills for many months. However, the island-hopping phase of the Pacific War really was over. Only one island now remained, and that was the one that everyone dreaded: Japan itself.

There was news from Europe, too. A big conference was being held at Potsdam between the "Big Three," which had been Stalin, Roosevelt, and Churchill but was now Stalin, Truman, and Churchill for a while (but then Atlee, because Churchill lost his re-election). Truman told Stalin that we had developed a new weapon of vast power, but was a little taken aback when Stalin seemed unimpressed, only remarking that he hoped we would "make good use of it."

Little did we know that Stalin had had spies in the Manhattan Project for years and knew everything he needed to know.

At Wendover Army Air Base on the Utah-Nevada border, a group of pilots and crew members had been training intensively for a special job that would require some very precise flying. They were flying modified and carefully maintained B-29 bombers, and security was as tight as possible.

Just to make sure that everyone knew security was no joke and that the leaders were deadly serious when they told the men they were not to talk about what they were doing or speculate about it out loud, several men who had the bad judgment to do so found themselves suddenly on their way to the Aleutian Islands, probably to a little garden spot called Shemya, a gloomy, frigid island where they would spend the rest of the war watching the snow and fog blow by.

The group of intensely trained airmen in Utah were about to take their special airplanes out to the Pacific, where they would soon visit the Japanese cities of Hiroshima and Nagasaki.

Admiral McCain's fleet was sailing up and down the Japanese coast, bombing airfields where kamikazes were based and actually going in so close that the battleships could hit factories with their big guns. Then they got an order to sail away, to stay clear of the coast until further notice. I've never read anything about it, but I imagine that if any of the sailors were looking back toward Japan on the morning of August 6, they would have been amazed by the extremely bright light they saw. That was Hiroshima, and though it took a while to realize it, the world's history had started down a new road.

The news naturally created a tremendous buzz among all Americans, young and old. Nobody really had a handle on what an "atomic bomb" was or how it worked, and the vague descriptions in the newspapers were often wrong. I think a lot of people soon gave up trying to understand it, but there were some of us who remained fascinated by the subject.

Then a few days later, another atomic bomb was dropped on Nagasaki, and there were some awesome pictures in the newspapers of the mushroom cloud over that city. The huge wave of excitement sweeping the U.S. grew even greater. Now it suddenly seemed that the Japs would *have* to surrender, either that or be wiped out completely, for now we finally had the means to totally annihilate them. A great feeling of relief swept over all Americans, especially those who would have had to do the invading, the Marines in particular. But the soldiers and the sailors knew that they, too, had just received a new lease on life and could actually start thinking about having a future.

A few more days passed, with a lot of bureaucratic jabber by the politicians, and then the surrender was finally official and the war was over. When the news broke, it was late afternoon, and I was given one of Mom's cooking pots, which I took up on top of an outcrop in the quarry and beat on with a big cooking spoon, putting many dents in it. One car with some people in it drove by; they looked at me strangely. Then we all piled into our car and went down to the main part of town, where there was a big crowd celebrating. About all I remember of that is an angry, sweating fat man with a short cigar in his mouth, looking hurried and hassled, trying to set off some skyrockets. He succeeded in this, but then he quickly went away, giving the impression that he urgently had to set off more rockets somewhere else and was already late.

CHAPTER 32

War Surplus

So the war had ended, but for a while nothing changed. Mom was able to trash the ration-stamp books. (Thankfully, she saved a few as memorabilia, and they are now part of my collection of "useless junk.") Soon the stores filled up with things to buy that had been impossible to find before. There were big stacks of tires at gas stations, and there were plenty of gasoline, shoes, and cigarettes. The meat crisis ended and there was plenty of meat to buy.

After a while, the newspapers and radio news started to fill up with stories about how bad things were in Europe. "Starving European" became a sort of catch phrase, and we kids used it now and then in ways we thought were humorous. Another phrase we heard a lot was "displaced person" or "D.P." for short. It seemed that Europe was filled with people, millions and millions of people, who didn't know where to go, couldn't go back to their homeland, or saw no point in trying to.

Even in England things were still bad, and they had been one of the victors! But it soon became obvious that the war was going to have to be paid for, and it had cost a *lot*. Rationing was kept in force in England for several years, and much of what you might call the "wartime spirit" went away. The "Let's all help each other out" sentiment gave way to one of "Look out for number one first."

There was a lot of talk about the atom bomb now, all the time. I had a few friends who were as fascinated as I was by the subject, and we all tried hard to get our hands on anything that revealed how it worked and what an atomic bomb actually *looked* like. That, the question of its physical appearance, was fascinating—a big secret that remained a secret for a long, long time. There were many rumors.

I had decided that I wanted to be a nuclear physicist, but later on, owing to a distinct lack of mathematical aptitude, I thought better of that idea.

Sometime during the summer of 1945, a twin-engine bomber, a B-25, trying to find Mitchel Field in the fog, flew into the Empire State Building at about the seventy-ninth floor. Firefighters had to go up about nine hundred feet carrying hoses. We heard about it on the radio, and I went up on the cliff to see if I could see it, but the clouds were too low to see anything. The crash did mess up the floor it hit pretty badly, and there was a fire, but it wasn't huge and didn't last very long. The Empire State Building was built with a rugged steel interior skeleton. There was never any danger of the building collapsing.

During that fall, my father's parents came to visit us, and I remember hearing my grandfather say to my father, "C'mon, Lloyd, let's split an atom!" meaning "Let's have a drink." Which must have been the "in" thing to say in Washington at the time.

War surplus stores sprang up in many places, and they were just chockablock full of all sorts of neat stuff. They were also called Army-Navy stores. You could find gloves, socks, shirts, pants, canteens, knives, compasses, sweaters, field jackets, K rations, C rations, Navy Pea Jackets, even parachutes—just about anything you could imagine, all for amazingly low prices. I bought a set of green-tinted plastic "snow-blindness goggles," with an elastic strap and fake fur around the edge, for only ten cents! They were not much good and I only tried them once, but hey, *ten cents*!

There was a huge cylindrical gas tank on the horizon, down in Newark. It looked as if it were as tall as the biggest buildings in the city. You couldn't see the sign painted on it from where we lived, but when you rode the train in or went anywhere near Newark in a car, you would see the gigantic sign painted on it in red white and blue that said, "Welcome Home, Boys." I believe that sign stayed up for many years.

The marvelous new insecticide DDT had been in use by the military for some time and had evidently done wonders for mosquito control in various tropical locations. Following the war, it started to appear in sprays available to civilians, and we got some. The first ones we had were called "bug bombs." They were red, about six or eight inches long, round at both ends with a valve at one end that you twisted to start or stop the spray. I figured that I would finally get those mosquitoes once and for all by fogging the air in my room so thick that they couldn't possibly avoid it. Well, I fogged it all right. I fogged it so thick that I could see only a yellow glow where the ceiling light was. That was probably too much.

DDT may have been used to try to control the mosquitoes that lived in the Jersey Meadows, but if so, it was many years before there was any noticeable improvement. They would still be there to keep you company in your room at night for a long time to come.

Changes in the world were becoming increasingly evident. Stories about discharged servicemen who were having trouble adjusting to civilian life began appearing in the news. "Crazed Vet Runs Amok" appeared as a typical newspaper headline in a Bill Maulden cartoon, and he also wrote about wives who were a little freaked out by their returned husbands sleeping with bayonets or loaded pistols under their pillows at night "because it just made them feel better." There was news of strikes, too. Now that the war was over and price controls were lifted, it seemed like all the big unions, one after another, went on strike to get more money. President Truman didn't like that and finally stomped them pretty hard, much harder than FDR ever had. People began to realize that the new president was not to be trifled with.

As I remember it, we kids had the opinion (absorbed from conversations around the dinner table) that the unions were just holding up the nation's progress and keeping us from getting back to the good times. Furthermore, calling a coal strike in the middle of winter was definitely *not* a good idea if you wanted people with coal-fired heat (a lot of us) to be sympathetic to your cause.

A building boom started almost immediately because there were now millions of servicemen returning to civilian life and starting families. My father was happy because it looked like he was going to have a lot of business. But restrictions were placed on building materials and it was mandated that half the material had to go into building houses worth less than $10,000. My father and his two partners wanted to build garden apartments, which cost a lot more than that.

Around this time, my father would bring home unusual items occasionally. One of them was a surplus weather balloon that we blew up with the vacuum cleaner hose. Then we had a six-foot white balloon in the living room and wondered what to do with it. I think there was a plan to paint something on it, and a face may have actually resulted, but I don't remember anything ever being done with it. One thing it did teach us was that it is not a good idea to let go of a monster balloon in the living room . . .

Another unusual item was a game played with a wide piece of paper about six feet long that had a number of parallel lines drawn on it, each line about an eighth of an inch wide. The lines were drawn with some chemical that burned like a fuse when lit. They all converged at the start point, so when a lit cigarette was pressed onto that point, the smoldering lines would all diverge and start advancing across the paper. It was supposed to be a horse race, you see, and each family member would have picked their own horse. It was a lot of fun, very exciting! But once it was over, you couldn't do it again; you had to have a new sheet. We only played it a few more times, I think. Maybe the sheets cost too much.

A book appeared on a small table in the living room around this time. I think it was the book my mother's reading club was reading for a while, but it stayed on that table for many, many years. In all those years I never picked it up to investigate it. I didn't like the look of the cover, which seemed ugly and depressing to me. It was a dirty yellow color with just a small splash of black across it and in the black patch, in small, hard-to-read red letters was the book's title. It was *Out of Africa*.

A thing that I had a lot of trouble understanding was why Russia did not seem to be friendly with us any more. Stories about them not cooperating with us and being purposely difficult became more and more frequent. I think that most kids felt like they didn't know what they were doing.

"What are they, crazy?" we would say. "Don't they know we can just squash them any time we want to? All it's gonna take is a few atom bombs, and then maybe Ivan will stop making so much trouble."

It was all very confusing, and I had a big problem adjusting to the change in our countries' relationship. It took several years for me to get over thinking of Russia as our big, crude, tough friend. I just couldn't understand why they wanted to make trouble.

But Churchill knew.

For a while after the war, I think we kids felt like America owned the world, and that we could run it and set up a system (run by us of course) in which nobody ever went hungry, and life was fair for everybody, "with liberty and justice for all."

We had a huge army and an air force and navy that were second to none, far bigger and better than anyone else's. Of all the nations actively involved in the fighting, we alone had not been injured by the war; it had only made us immensely rich and powerful . . . and dangerous. We felt like it was time for us to take over and run things. "And if anyone tries to make trouble, why, just rap them once, *BLAP!* across the nose."

That's what some of us thought.

Now, I think it's a good thing we didn't try it. We really aren't smart enough. We would have only made a worse mess of things.

Maybe even worse than what has actually happened.

1946

CHAPTER 33

Full Circle: Another Battleship

The year 1946 wasn't really a war year; it was more like a long hangover. The war was still ringing in our ears.

Bing Crosby recorded a song called "The Big Movie Show in the Sky," which was a big hit. It had been intended for release in 1945, but the war ended too soon. The song seemed to ask a man in the Pacific theater if he could be unashamed of his life if asked to account for it now. That was a good song.

Still is. "By and by . . . by and by . . . can you look yourself in the eye?" Good message.

There was another song that came out around this time about the Atchison, Topeka, and Santa Fe railroad, and it was a very catchy tune. For a while we all were singing it, at least the chorus, which went, oddly enough: "The Atchison, Topeka, and the Santa Faaaaay!"

Seems to me it resembled "Chattanooga Choo Choo" a lot, but that might just be because they were both about railroads.

I don't remember whether or not the girls in sixth grade were wearing saddle shoes and bobby sox (probably most had been forbidden to because they were too young to be so daring), but their older sisters certainly were. Sweaters, too, but "Sweater Girls" were also thought to be pretty daring, and some girls' mothers made them wear things called "dickies" under their sweaters, which made them appear more flat-chested. Very strange.

I was outraged when the price of a pack of gum or lifesavers went up to six cents after being a nickel all through the war. That was the first time we felt inflation's bite, and it has never let up since.

Some sort of competition involving an obstacle course was held by the

Boy Scouts. The obstacle course started on Valley Road (near the place where we had bought pumpkins) and went straight up the side of the Watchung ridge. I had always thought I was very good at obstacle courses, because I was always doing things like climbing in the quarry or running in the woods. I don't remember whether it was supposed to be a real race or not, but it seemed to turn into one. The competitors took off on the course, and about halfway up, I was surprised to hear someone approach me fast from behind, then pass me and forge ahead, scrambling like mad. I tried hard, but I couldn't quite catch him. It was Charlie Martin again.

Sometime—I think it must have been in early spring, because it was pretty chilly—elements of the fleet came to New York Harbor again, and my parents took Charlie and me in to see it. This was sure not the same fleet we had visited six years before. These were great, dark, serious-looking ships, ships that had been to war. One of them, I think it was the aircraft carrier *Franklin*, had been fire-blackened in several places and still showed much of the battle damage she had received, with a great, gaping hole in the flight deck and blistered sides where fires had burned. She had been the most seriously damaged ship to come home all the way across the Pacific under her own power.

I suppose they wanted to show her off, to show the civilians that it had not been all fun and games for the navy either.

We went to see the USS *Missouri*, the ship where the surrender ceremony had been held. That vast, sweeping, dark-gray mountain of steel, 288 feet longer and 20,000 tons more massive than the USS *New York*, which had impressed me so in 1939, seemed looming and serious. There was no question that this was a machine for war. And there, set in the deck, was the shining golden circle, the polished bronze plate that marks the spot where the surrender was signed. I think it had a low rope around it, suspended on stanchions. I looked around, then bent down and touched the golden circle, and it was then that I realized that the war that I had lived with and that had shaped most of my life was truly over.

The war was finally really finished.

And now, since this story was intended tell what it was like to be a kid during World War II, I guess it's finished too.

Plant ya now, dig ya later.

www.ingramcontent.com/pod-product-compliance
Lightning Source LLC
Chambersburg PA
CBHW022008090426
42741CB00007B/941